NIRVANA

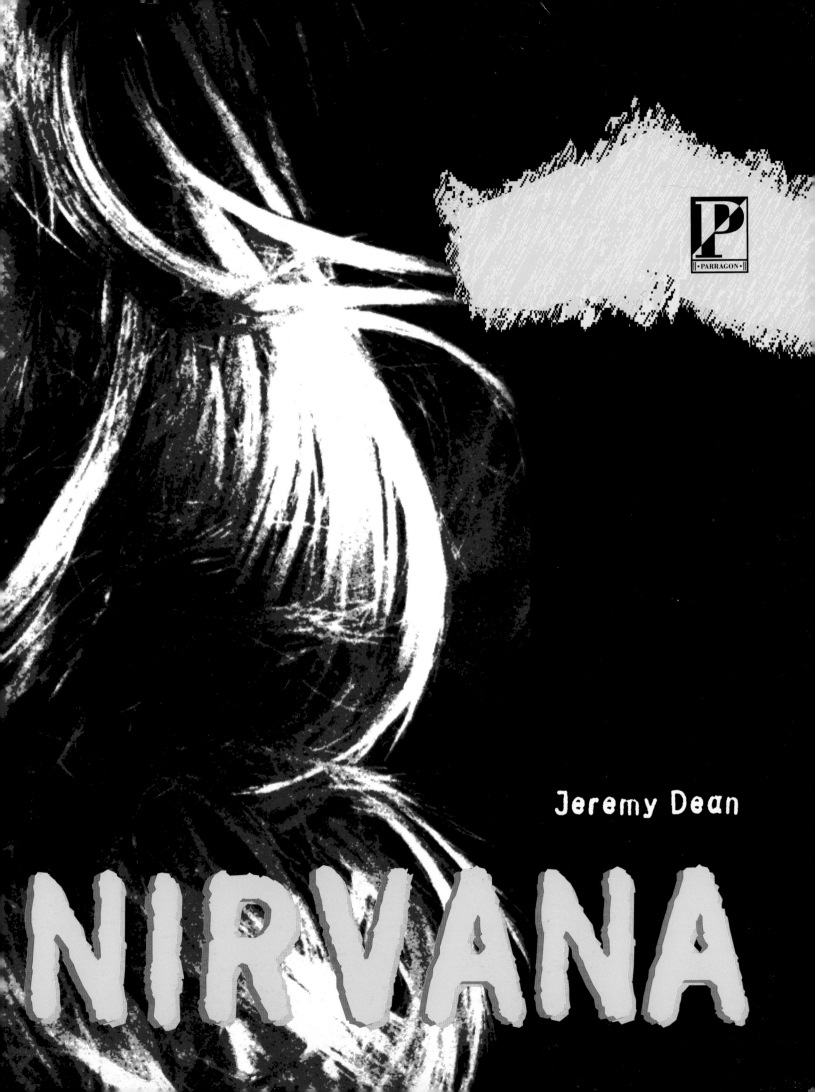

This edition published 1996 by
Parragon Book Service Ltd
Unit 13-17 Avonbridge Trading Estate,
Atlantic Rd, Avonmouth
Bristol BS11 9QD

Produced by Carlton Books
20 St. Anne's Court
London W1V 3AW

Text and design copyright © 1996 Carlton Books Limited

ISBN 0.75251.860.7

Printed and bound in Italy

Acknowledgements
The publishers would like to thank the following sources for their kind permission to reproduce
the pictures in this book.

All Action/Justin Thomas; Corbis-Bettmann/UPI; Hulton Getty; London Features
International/Matt Anker, Kristin Callahan, Paul Canty, George De Sota, Gie Knaeps, Kevin
Mazur, Tim Paton, Geoff Swaine; Pictorial Press/Hanne Jordan, Jeffrey Mayer; Retna/Steve
Double, Steve Gullick, Niels Van Iperen, Steve Pyke, Ed Sirrs, Steve Sweet, Chris Taylor, Ian
Tilton, Chris Toliver, Alice Wheeler; Rex Features/SIPA; S.I.N/David Anderson, Peter Anderson,
Richard Beland, Stewart Cook, Steve Double, Martyn Goodacre, Ian Lawton, Don Lewis, Tony
Mott, Tim Owen, Tim Paton, Phil Nicholls, Peter Noble, Roy Tee, Ian Tilton.

Every effort has been made to acknowledge correctly and contact the source and/or copyright
holder of each picture, and Carlton Books Limited apologises for any unintentional errors or
omissions which will be corrected in future editions of the book.

CONTENTS

CHAPTER 1

Tortured & Tender Poet......................6

CHAPTER 2

Nevermind the Grunge......................30

CHAPTER 3

A Little Habit......................54

CHAPTER 4

Love is Tough......................78

CHAPTER 5

Never Fade Away......................102

DISCOGRAPHY......................**118**

CHRONOLOGY......................**125**

INDEX......................**127**

TORTURED & TENDER POET

Nirvana is the ultimate goal of Buddhism. A state of Nirvana is achieved by attaining freedom from all limitations of both existence and rebirth. This is done through the overcoming and eradication of all desires. Nirvana can also mean the negation of the mundane, a spiritual release, the end of reincarnation, union with God or oneness with the Absolute...

It is a hard thing to define — if it can be a thing at all — and even harder to achieve. Then again it is, in itself, perfectly simple and may come with your next breath...

To millions of people throughout the western world, the term Nirvana means something quite different, but has been equally profound to many.

The year of 1991 heralded a new decade, which would also be the last of the millennia. As always at the end of an era and the dawning of a new age, people looked around themselves to find some fresh meaning. For many of America's youth, that meaning was embodied in a song with the title 'Smells Like Teen Spirit'. The band called themselves Nirvana — they achieved it and lost it. Their story is laced with, lies, success, drama, money, sex, drugs and tragedy. Their legacy is a music with vast and enduring appeal that will continue to assert a major influence on the rock world well into the age of Aquarius.

Anyone who can recall the first time they heard the breakthrough single 'Smells Like Teen Spirit' will remember the instant hook that pulled them in and the astonishment at the freshness, energy and sheer appeal of the sound. It was all the things that pop should be, as well as alternative, punk, metal and heavy rock. Something for everyone and everything for some. It seemed to have come from nowhere, but of course it did come from somewhere. It came from a the decade-long heritage of punk tradition, and the creativity of three driven musicians, one of them a tortured and tender poet...

Nirvana live — on hands experience

Kurt Donald Cobain was born in Hoquiam near Aberdeen, Washington, to Wendy and Donald on February 20, 1967. He was to die on April 5, 1994.

Kurt was a bright and receptive young boy who expressed an interest in music from the early age of two. He beat his Micky Mouse drum to the radiogram records of The Monkees and the Beatles — demonstrating even then that he had an ear for music and melody and that his ear needed to be nurtured. Kurt's maternal aunt, Mary, gave the young boy his first guitar lessons, but found that he would not sit still and concentrate, pretty much as any six or seven would not.

His parents wasted little time in taking Kurt to see specialists who agreed that he was hyperactive, a term that is often used to describe inquisitive, enthusiastic and intelligent children. He was prescribed Ritalin, a type of amphetamine which helps to counter hyperactivity. This was the beginning of a life of drug use, abuse and dependence for Kurt.

In 1975, Kurt's parents divorced. It caused a great deal of stress and anguish to the eight-year-old Kurt; when his parents split up, he had to go and live with his mother. It was around this time that he was first diagnosed as suffering from an array of allergies, mainly to food additives, which aggravated his sensitive stomach and were said to cause behavioral problems.

He lived with his mother for the first year after the split. When she became more seriously involved with a new boyfriend, Kurt was packed off to his father's trailer, pitched in a park in Montesano. Kurt was later to recall, in interviews, how unhappy he had been, even in his youth. 'I had a really good childhood up until I was nine,' he explained, 'then a classic case of divorce really affected me and I moved back and forth between relatives all the time. And I just became extremely depressed and withdrawn.'

Kurt Cobain, the child — happy days (before the daze)

Kurt's father, Donald, was to remarry a year later in the February of 1978. Kurt found himself in the middle of a new, ready-made family. Same dad, new mother and siblings. He had already become far more quiet and withdrawn and this sense of being 'spare baggage' may have contributed to the feelings of alienation so well expressed throughout his later works and suicide notes.

Kurt had been finding expression for his inner emotions through music. First by listening to and empathizing with bands like Black Sabbath, David Bowie and later the Sex Pistols — who he had admired for some time before he actually got to hear a record by them. Kurt got his first guitar for his fourteenth birthday in 1981. He keenly attended guitar lessons and practised for many hours alone in his room.

While attending Montesano High School, he first met Buzz Osbourne and Matt Lukin who played with a then

small-time local band, The Melvins. 'My life was really boring,' commented Cobain, 'All of a sudden, I found a totally different world. I started getting into music and finally seeing shows and doing the things I always wanted to do while I was in high school.'

Also attending the High School was a young immigrant by the name of Chris Novoselic — a friend of Dale Crover — who later became the drummer for The Melvins. Chris was older, but shared Kurt's strange and outrageous sense of humour. The more Kurt mixed with the circle around The Melvins and the local scene, the more he began to get on with Chris, or Krist as he would later become known.

Krist Novoselic was born to parents Krist and Maria on May 16, 1965. The family name of Novoselic is derived from the Croatian term meaning a 'new settler'.

When he was aged around twelve in 1979, he moved with his family to the town of Aberdeen, Washington. He hardly had a chance to settle into his new surroundings, school and circle of potential friends before he was sent away to live with relatives in Croatia, in the June of 1980. He was to spend a year living in the land of his fathers before returning to Aberdeen to complete his schooling, and graduate in 1983. Around this difficult period, Krist's parents also separated.

HOMO SEX RULES

For Kurt it had all happened at an earlier age, and his adolescence was spent moving between the care of grandparents and different aunts and uncles until he moved back in with his mother at the age of seventeen. Kurt's mother, Wendy, had remarried in May 1984, when she was wed to Patrick O'Connor. Kurt once again found himself acting as a reminder of things gone by, and distanced himself by becoming immersed in the new punk ethic and lifestyle.

Drugs were easy to come by among the sensation-seeking youth of a lacklustre town. He was soon smoking hash and trying out any kick that came his way. Kurt had been experimenting with drugs and substances for some time, probably developing from the drugs he was

> # "I had a really good childhood up until I was nine, then a classic case of divorce really affected me."
>
> ## KURT COBAIN

prescribed as a child — self medication in a way... He is known to have tried heroin by the summer of 1986, and he continued experimenting with hard drugs throughout his life.

He was arrested for vandalism when he graffitied 'Homo Sex Rules' on the wall of a bank. A close friend of Kurt's at school turned out to be gay, and this had made their continued friendship impossible in the midst of redneck, logging-town, low-brow intolerance.

His love of music and his quickly growing creative abilities gave him the impetus at the age of eighteen to leave full-time education, dropping out of school just

"I have a problem with the average macho man — they've always been a threat to me."

KURT COBAIN

He moved from friend to friend, sleeping on floors and sometimes in the street or sheltering under a bridge. He eventually began moving further afield to the nearby town of Olympia where he found a tight artistic community which seemed to be more right-on and positive than what he had come to expect from the bored youth of Aberdeen. This kool kulture surrounded the local K Records label and the bands it showcased. Kurt was attracted to the K ideology and later gave himself a home-made tattoo of the label's logo. It was among this circle in Olympia that he met, and moved in, with Tracy Marander. They shared their modest apartment with a variety of beasts including a parrot, three rabbits and a tank of terrapins.

FECAL MATTER TO COCK-ROCK

Kurt had also become friends with local musician Buzz Osbourne of The Melvins. It was Buzz who introduced Kurt to the new wave of US punkers with bands like Black Flag, The Dead Kennedys and Flipper. Kurt tried out for becoming the guitarist for The Melvins, but lacked the confidence at the time to show the full potential of his playing. Kurt had been helping out a few local bands as a 'roadie' but was a particular fan and supporter of The Melvins.

The first band proper with whom Kurt played was endearingly called Fecal Matter, and featured Greg Hokanson on drums and Dale Crover, who was drummer in The Melvins, on bass guitar. They played a few very small live gigs themselves and a few more supporting The Melvins, eventually recording a demo tape but splitting up shortly afterwards. Song titles on the demo included 'Sound of Dentage', 'Laminated Effect' and 'Downer' the instrumental which later resurfaced on the *Bleach* album.

An ex-school colleague of Kurt's, Krist Novoselic, was reintroduced by Buzz and a friendship developed. Kurt

weeks short of graduation and passing up two offers of art scholarships. He had decided that he was destined to be involved in some aspect of music. He started being a roadie for The Melvins. He learned much by just watching and talking with them. Kurt began pursuing his own musical ambitions, albeit in a rather haphazard way, while working in any dead-end job he could land. His first was a brief stint as a janitor. Then he found himself working in a dental surgery, as a swimming instructor and as a hotel cleaner. He took the job in the hotel so he might have access to vacant rooms on nights when he had nowhere else to sleep.

Kurt was later to comment, 'I always wanted to move to the big city. I wanted to move to Seattle, sell my ass, and be a punk rocker, but I was too afraid. So I just stayed in Aberdeen for too long... until I was twenty years old.'

Something for everyone — everything to some

had been sending Krist — or Chris as he was still more usually known then — tapes of his Fecal Matter material. Shortly after the demise of Fecal Matter, in the winter of 1986, Krist and Kurt decided to form a band themselves. They began rehearsing with Robert McFadden, an acquaintance who owned a drum kit. The chemistry was not there and after only one month Bob McFadden left Krist and Kurt, who continued writing and rehearsing as a duo, with occasional help from Dale Crover and Mike Dillard on drums.

Dale Crover and Buzz Osbourne, from The Melvins, also used Kurt on guitar and lead vocals in a short lived band called Brown Cow. Kurt and Krist got together again and went through various combinations with other musicians for a group they called Stiff Woodies before settling on a three-man band with Steve Newman on bass,

Kurt Cobain, the man (with the child in his eyes...)

The Melvins: Kurt would never come to terms with being bigger than the heroes of his youth.

called The Sellouts. Newman tragically lost some fingers in a later accident with a chainsaw.

For a short time Krist and Kurt continued as a duo, using Bob McFadden on drums for rehearsals. It soon became clear that Kurt was the writer of the two, and they built a repertoire around Kurt's material. In April 1987 they recruited Aaron Burckhard on drums and took their songs to the public in the form of several live gigs in local venues. This was the line-up that was to eventually become the first incarnation of Nirvana. To begin with, they were

As far back as high school, Chris (Krist) and Kurt shared a strange sense of humour.

"I **wanted** to move to Seattle, sell my **ass**, and be a **punk rocker**, but I was too **afraid**. So I just stayed in **Aberdeen** for too long... until I was **twenty** years old."

KURT COBAIN

ironically named Skid Row, not to be confused with the popular cock-rock outfit of the same name! They went through a colourful variety of other identities before settling on the name: Ted Ed Fred, Bliss, Throat Oyster, Pen Cap Chew, Windowpane... Nirvana. The songs they were showcasing included 'Floyd The Barber', 'Aero Zeppelin', 'Beeswax' written by Cobain, and a cover of Dutch band Shocking Blue's song, 'Love Buzz'. A live session for local radio station KAOS became their first demo.

There had been two bands before them to be called Nirvana, one was a one-hit group from the early Sixties, and the second was a pro-Christian group who actually tried to sue Cobain and Co.

PUNK ROCK BAND SEEKS DRUMMER

It was 1988 when Nirvana made their first studio demo, with Dale Crover on percussion. The tape was recorded at Seattle's Reciprocal Recording studio, run by up and coming Seattle-based producer Jack Endino. It cost them $152.44 [£98.35] and consisted of ten tracks. Most of the tracks

1992 — serious success!

included in this demo appeared on the debut album and four went on to finally appear, four years later, on the *Incesticide* LP, in 1992.

They sent their demo tape to a number of record labels that had signed US punk bands they particularly admired. Those labels included Touch & Go, SST and Alternative Tentacles. Their break actually came when Jack Endino passed a copy of their tape to Bruce Pavitt and Jonathan Poneman, label bosses at Seattle's Sub Pop record label. On the strength of the demo, they attended one of Nirvana's gigs at the Central Tavern, Seattle and later arranged a meeting with Kurt and Krist. As a result, they were invited to record a track for a forthcoming Sub Pop compilation showcase album.

By this time Dale Crover was too busy with his own projects and The Melvins to devote enough time to Nirvana's busier and busier schedule. Kurt and Krist decided

1989, Hoboken, NY: Nirvana with pal, Jason Everman (left), who joined their live line-up.

The chord that broke the guitar's back: Kurt had been abusing instruments since 1988.

it was now time to recruit a full-time drummer of their own and so placed an advert in the local Rocket paper. The ad read: 'Heavy, light punk rock band: Aerosmith, Led Zeppelin, Black Sabbath, Black Flag, Scratch Acid, Butthole Surfers. Seeks drummer.' Out of the potentials and hopefuls that replied to the classified, Chad Channing was the successful applicant who joined the line-up to record a batch of tracks with Endino at Reciprocal on June 11, 1988. The tracks included 'Love Buzz' and 'Big Cheese'.

Chad Channing was born to Wayne and Burnyce on January 31, 1967 in Santa Rosa, California. Like all the main members of Nirvana, and a high percentage of contemporary American youth, he was a product of a broken home after his parents divorced. Kurt and Krist first

17

"The Bay City Rollers after an assault by Black Sabbath."

KURT COBAIN ON THE SOUND OF NIRVANA

1990, New York City: back to the three-piece line-up and teetering on the verge of success.

saw him showcase his drumming skill when he was playing in a band called Tick-Dolly-Row alongside Ben Shepherd, who went on to become bass player with Soundgarden.

'Spank Thru' — recorded on September 27 — was selected for inclusion on the *Sub Pop 200* compilation. Nirvana were already becoming a name in the live Seattle scene and Kurt Cobain put fuel to the fire with more and more confident and energetic stage antics. He destroyed his first guitar on October 30 at a well-attended Seattle venue.

Shortly after, Sub Pop released Nirvana's debut single, 'Love Buzz'/'Big Cheese' as a limited edition of just one thousand, each numbered by hand. The cover listed the band members and misspelled Kurdt Kobain. The origin of this wrong spelling of Kurt's name has been traced to the track 'Mexican Seafood', which they contributed to a Caroline Records compilation, *Teriyaki Asthma*. It is said that when they were putting together the liner notes, the people at the record company were unsure of the spelling and so consulted the person who they thought should know. Obviously, thinking of another stem language for the name, that person completely misspelled the name... The original pressings of the 'Love Buzz' limited edition now change hands for around £200.

BLEACHED

Nirvana began recording sessions for an LP for Sub Pop the day before Christmas 1988 and continued through into the New Year, finishing the recording for *Bleach* on January 24, 1989. The album emerged as a concoction made up from various elements taken from Seventies pop rock, spunky punk and distempered metal. Kurt Cobain once described their sound as being like 'The Bay City Rollers after an assault by Black Sabbath'. Bleach was recorded on a very tight budget, and total studio costs ended up around £400! This surprisingly small sum was paid for by Jason Everman, a good friend of Kurt and Krist and an ex-school pal of Chad's.

Sub Pop liked what Nirvana delivered in so short a time and at so low a cost, and set them up for their first major US tour. The label delayed the release of the album so that two old songs, 'Paper Cuts' and 'Floyd The Barber', taken directly from the original demo tape with Dale Crover, could be added. The label also demanded that the tracks be resequenced. Although the promotional tour was in February, with Jason Everman joining the live line-up on guitar, Bleach was not released until June 1989. A more

major US tour, the first extensive tour for Nirvana, started on June 22 at the Covered Wagon in San Francisco. For each date on that tour, Nirvana were paid around £65 and a crate of beer. They drove from venue to venue in a small tour van and gradually the tension of touring took its toll. They began drinking more and more before taking the stage, and were soon releasing their tension and frustrations by trashing the gear onstage. It has been surmised that this behaviour started out as a parody of Jason Everman's stadium rock attitude and antics, it is known that he did not fit in too well with the otherwise pop-punk approach of Nirvana and appeared to be more suited to a heavy metal band and audience.

Head-bangers' ball

Introduce yourselves: (L-R) Kurt Cobain, Krist Novoselic, Chad Channing — we are Nirvana!

Nirvana's live shows were everything that rock'n'roll wants to be.

In those early days Nirvana tours were far from the rock cliché of limousines and trashed hotel rooms. They usually had to appeal to strangers at the end of gigs to allow them to crash out on their floor. One night, after a gig in Texas, when this tactic had not paid off, they found themselves sleeping under the stars. They had chosen a nice quiet spot by the side of a lake, but found it difficult to sleep. Maybe they found the 'Beware: Alligators' signs a little off-putting...

The tour was cut short in mid July when Jason Everman left to join fellow Seattle rockers, Soundgarden. He also played with Mindfunk and eventually signed up with the US Navy in 1994 — not a very grunge or punk thing to do, maybe, but marginally more productive than some other's chosen exit that same year. Whether it is nobler in the mind to train to kill others with big weapons or simply kill yourself with a shotgun? That could be the

20

question… but the answer would always come up that only one option is reversible if things change.

THE VOICE OF DISCONTENT

Bleach was well received by the local punk fans, who were attracted by its distinctively Sub Pop rough and ready appeal. The simple cover proudly displayed a gritty black and white photograph of the band in live, full-on rock-out action. The photo was taken by Tracy Marander, Kurt's girlfriend at the time. The other photos on the packaging were by photographer Charles Peterson, who had been providing most of the characteristic cover shots for Sub Pop's releases. Capturing the atmosphere of Seattle's sweaty punk venues with their hard-moshing audiences and hard-playing bands, Peterson's pictures were instrumental in importing the feel of punk to the kids in America. The feel

Hoser couture

"There's like a collective unconsciousness there. Just people in their houses, drinking a lot. A lot of drugs."

KRIST NOVOSELIC ON ABERDEEN

of Sub Pop's sounds and images became the style guide for what was to be branded 'grunge', the brand standard for the new generic voice of the generation. Little did they know at that time what Nirvana were truly capable of or that Kurt Cobain would become that generation's foremost spokesperson and voice of discontent.

The sound of Nirvana on *Bleach* was a refreshing amalgam of more mainstream, middle of the road American rock sensibilities with the new ascerbic punker ethic. In other words, the songs were kinda catchy, but pretty thrashy. Kurt's lyrics were obscure much of the time, but tended to deal with his personal views on the scene surrounding him. An outsider's view of the new Seattle art-punk pretensions and the road to mass acceptability

that was being paved. A road which Nirvana intended to travel along in the fast lane, entirely of their own volition, while attempting to retain some integrity and punk philosophy. Kurt believed that Nirvana had the potential to appeal to more than just the alternative metal audiences and wanted to take his songs across the mainstream to the Top 40 bank. This is, of course what he achieved, though we were later to realize that he himself believed he had failed, thinking that his audience felt betrayed.

The song which most overtly dealt with the contemporary Seattle scene is 'School', which compares the new wave of 'grunge' bands to high school cliques. Other songs were drawn from life, and were even biographical, such as 'About A Girl' which is about a girl called Tracy Marander, his current girlfriend, who apparently threatened to throw him out if he did not land a job. 'Scoff' is a jibe, a 'So there!' to all those who had lacked confidence in his ability and dismissed his musical ambitions as pie-in-the-sky pipe dreams. 'Big Cheese' is a song about the pressures people are put under to please the boss, be it a factory worker under the foreman, or a new band under demanding label bosses. 'Paper Cuts' tackles the touchy subject of parental neglect and the lyrics carry references to a real family that Kurt had known, who used to lock their children in a room for punishment. 'Floyd The Barber' is about the rot of subsurface paranoia and psychosis behind the all-American facade of small-town USA. In a David Lynch-style vignette, the characters in the song turn out to be murderers. 'Negative Creep' is a character portrait of an

'Out of all the bands who came from the underground and actually made it in the mainstream, Devo is the most subversive and challenging of all.' Kurt Cobain

unhappy, antisocial individual and certainly contains elements of self-effacement. The other songs from the album are more abstract but based around specific themes. 'Blew' explores entrapment, being in a rut and afraid to get out. 'Swap Meet' is a comment on the attractions and differences between the sexes, what unites and divides. 'Mr Moustache' is a satire of macho male stereotypes. 'Sifting' is antiauthoritarian.

TO EUROPE

Nirvana restructured their live show as a three-piece and continued a series of US dates later in 1989, through August and September. Around this time they also enlisted the talents of producer Steve Fisk to record the *Blew* EP.

Meat Puppets. Often covered by Nirvana at live gigs.

The US tour ran on into their first European tour, jointly headlining with established Seattle rock outfit, Tad. *Bleach* had been released in Europe by Tupelo Records in late August. The first Euro-date, promoting the debut album, was in the UK at the Riverside, Newcastle, and a later date at London's School Of Oriental And African Studies was almost cancelled by British fire brigade officials when they found out that ticket sales exceeded the audience safety limit by more than twice as much!

Their live shows were everything that rock'n'roll wants to be. Their audiences were energized into a molten mass of sweaty moshers. Nirvana kicked butt big time. They were gathering the blooms from the seeds sown by more mainstream soft rockers and weaving them into pop garlands and rock wreaths. They were the culmination of everything that had gone before them.

Their major influences were probably obscure to many of their audience. They often opened their live sets with 'Molly's Lips', a cover version of a song by Scottish band The Vaselines. Nirvana covered other songs by The Vaselines including 'Jesus Didn't Want Me For A Sunbeam' and 'Son Of A Gun'. Other songs that were cover versions included: 'Return Of The Rat' and 'D-7', originally by The Wipers; 'Turnaround' by Devo; 'Lake Of Fire', 'Oh Me' and 'Plateau' by The Meat Puppets; 'Where Did You Sleep Last Night', by Leadbelly; and 'Money Will Roll Right In' by fellow Seattle contemporaries Mudhoney. 'Love Buzz', which had been their first single was, of course, a cover of Dutch band Shocking Blue.

Other groups they admired and paid tribute to by covering their songs were a little more obvious and well known. They paid homage to David Bowie by performing 'The Man Who Sold The World', and covered songs from the influential Velvet Underground. Also they played Kiss, 'Do You Love Me', and The Doors classic, 'The End', which carries an explicit theme of suicide.

Kurt seemed to suffer from increasing stress during the tour. Nirvana and Tad were sharing a tour bus and were not well matched in interests or attitudes. At one point during the tour, Kurt complained to Sub Pop's Jonathan Poneman that he had not formed a band to pander to the demands of what he perceived as bovine audiences. He was beginning to feel frustrated and misunderstood…

At the Rome date in November, Kurt scaled the PA speaker stack and threatened to jump off. Later he was seen in tears backstage. This was said to be the culmination of the slowly building stress and worsening stomach pain. Kurt confessed that he hated and wanted to kill his colleagues and that he would rather give up the band than continue. After some coaxing and calming from

"We played some kind of benefit show on a Sunday afternoon at the Central Tavern. We showed up, set up, and nobody was there."

KRIST NOVOSELIC ON PRE-BLEACH SEATTLE

Kiss: punk metal or glam rock — either way they have been quoted as an influence by purveyors of the new US alternative wave from Nine Inch Nails to Nirvana.

Velvet Underground: probably the most influential band in modern rock, fronted by Lou Reed, and here featuring Nico, (centre) from around the time of their legendary Andy Warhol album.

Jonathan Poneman, Kurt got over what had then seemed merely a minor tantrum. The tour continued.

PLOUGHING A NEW PLAYGROUND

At the end of the tour they returned to the UK to play Sub Pop's Lamefest at the London Astoria, on December 3. They were, by then, billed below Tad and Mudhoney. At the end of the Nirvana set, Kurt hurled his guitar at Krist in a gesture of sufferance. That was the fourth guitar to be smashed or damaged during the set.

Shortly following the tour's aftermath, Krist married his long-standing girlfriend, Shelli, in Tacoma, Washington, on December 30, 1989.

The next year, 1990, began with the Euro release of the *Blew* EP in January. The months that followed saw much turmoil and many changes in the state of Nirvana. Their label at the time, Sub Pop, was running into deeper difficulties on the cash front, and the band changed its line-up several times. Nirvana had been successfully marketed and a demand had been created for their music among the youth across USA. Independent record

"All I really had was a suitcase and my drums. So I took them up to Seattle and hoped it would work. It did."

DAVE GROHL

Dave Grohl, ex-Scream drummer joins up.

distribution systems in America made it almost impossible for the kids in some areas to get hold of copies of *Bleach*. Kurt and Krist were glad of the break afforded them by Sub Pop, but knew that the days of Nirvana were numbered unless they could get better distribution on a major label. Their contract was fairly flexible and although they had began work on a second album for Sub Pop, they found they only had to fulfil a promise of another single. They began putting out feelers

to some major labels and received some immediate interest from Columbia. This turned out to be unworkable and the interest petered out.

At a gig at New York's Pyramid club, two of Sonic Youth's core, Thurston Moore and Kim Gorden, were in the audience with associate, Gary Gersh, who was an A&R man for Dave Geffen's record label. Sonic Youth had then only recently signed to Geffen. Gersh was immediately impressed by Nirvana's obvious potential to break through big time.

At one gig in Portland, Oregon, around this time Kurt had met Courtney Love, of Hole, for the first time. Courtney described Nirvana's music as 'ploughing a new playground for us all to play in'.

27

> "I was **looking** for **something** a lot **heavier**, yet **melodic** at the same **time.** Something **different** from **heavy metal,** a different **attitude."**

KURT COBAIN

For a short while, Dale Crover restrained Kurt's violent onstage antics and guitar abuse, but the nemesis of frustration was never far from the surface

By April, Sub Pop were in obvious difficulties and several major labels were circling Nirvana, who had just recorded a seven-track demo with producer Butch Vig. Vig is the well-respected producer who has worked notably with Nine Inch Nails and went on to form the band Garbage. The demo began doing the rounds of majors, showcasing the more focused style of heavy-light musical counter pointing that was to become the Nirvana trade mark. Chad Channing did not fit with this new direction and was sacked from the band to be replaced, albeit briefly, by Mudhoney's drummer, Dan Peters. They recorded a new single, 'Sliver', for Sub Pop with this line-up, apparently taking less than an hour in the studio to do so!

They followed up the single with a seven date mini-tour of the West Coast, with Dale Crover stepping in on drums. By now, Nirvana's reputation for anarchic antics at live gigs had become widespread, but for this tour no equipment was smashed up or abused. This was, apparently, due to the specific request by Crover to abstain from that sort of behaviour while he was associated with the group.

Later, on September 22, they played the Seattle Motor Sports Show, their only gig to feature Dan Peters on percussion. In the audience was another young drummer who had been following Nirvana's development for some time. He was Dave Grohl from the Washington DC hardcore band Scream. Within the space of a month, Peters had been sacked to be replaced by Grohl. Both Krist and Kurt had been admirers of Grohl's abilities since seeing Scream perform, and it turned out that they had a mutual friend in Buzz Osbourne of The Melvins. Scream were in a lull at this time — their bassist had left the band without a trace or an explanation — and so Grohl took advantage of this period in limbo to fly to Seattle, with the encouragement of Osbourne, and test for Nirvana. He made his Nirvana live debut at Olympia's North Shore Surf Club in October before joining them on their joint European tour with L7.

NEVERMIND THE GRUNGE

David Eric Grohl was born to James and Virginia on January 14, 1969 in Warren, Ohio. He came from a musical background, his mother had been involved with singing in bands in her younger days and his father was an accomplished flautist. Music was in David's blood and for as long as he could remember there had always been a guitar to hand. His parents divorced when he was six. He did not seriously develop his musical talents until he was around ten years of age, when those around him insisted he take lessons as the only song he really knew how to play was 'Smoke On The Water', and everyone was sick of it. He did not get on with the traditional approach of his teachers and stopped taking lessons within the year. He preferred to develop his own style and learn to play by ear by mimicking Beatles' songs. As early as eleven, along with his friend Larry Hinkle, Dave was recording his own material, using a school cassette recorder.

For Christmas 1981, aged twelve, he acquired his first electric guitar, a stylish Sixties Silvertone model with a built-in amplifier. Dave was totally captivated by the new scope that the electric offered, he played it so much that by Spring it was broken and replaced by a black Les Paul Memphis copy. He joined a local band that did cover versions and performed at private parties, local high schools and nursing homes.

Dave was introduced to punk and new wave by a cousin he visited one summer, when he was thirteen. The year was 1982 and punk was still a subculture in the USA. His cousin, Tracy, had an extensive record collection including many European imports of UK punk bands and even some American bands that were not distributed in the USA. That same year, Dave went to his first live rock gig to see Naked Raygun and ROTA. He saw the bands onstage and began thinking that one day...

Punk never really happened in the USA, not in the same way it exploded across Europe, especially the UK and Germany in the late Seventies and early Eighties. The American record industry is dependent on complex distribution due to the country's vast size. Independent

Kurt smiles like teen spirit.

New wave punkers, like the Dead Kennedys, appealed to Kurt Cobain

labels have real difficulty in getting their records beyond local shops. Also getting air time on MTV is probably the most important factor for any rock record's sales. Some parts of the USA are so isolated from the happening centres of culture, that the only way their inhabitants would know that a band even existed would be seeing them on MTV. If a record label does not have major distribution and cannot get its bands played on MTV, it cannot reach the majority of America's potential record-buying public. The only alternative outlet is the college radio network.

In the UK around the punk era, things were very different. Small DIY record labels were made possible by the underground network of fanzines and because distribution was relatively easy. A band could record and release their own records and distribute them themselves. The only true punk band from America to gain

Sex Pistols sign the dotted line... anarchy goes commercial in the UK.

recognition in the punk explosion were the Dead Kennedys (and later some other bands sharing their Alternative Tentacles record label). In Europe it was much easier to have a small independent punk label than in America, and the overtly political and angry lyrics of the Dead Kennedys crossed cultural barriers. Although main man Jello Biafra was singing about American politics with a generally antigovernment message, the punks in the UK could still identify with the sentiment. After all, political themes like Vietnam and Cambodia, the bomb, or the rich exploiting the poor, are world problems and concern us all. News of the Dead Kennedys' success in Europe created interest in the USA and eventually US punk records were being shipped from Europe to the States.

In a way this phenomenon was puzzling. It was the early Eighties and punk was in its death throes, corrupted by corporate marketing and commercialization of punk styles, punk clothes and punk ethics. The increasingly

The new line-up.

right-wing British establishment stepped in and effectively rendered punk impotent by absorbing it into the consumer system, making it saleable, profitable, fashionable. In other words, UK punk became all the things that it opposed.

The real alternative scene was driven underground and punk developed into what was known as 'hardcore' back in the USA. It was this new strain of hardcore bands that began influencing the youth of America. Other bands carried by Alternative Tentacles were DOA, Black Flag, Millions Of Dead Cops and Husker Du, to name only a few. All these groups were seminal and important influences on the scene that was to break into the mainstream a decade later. That scene would become known as grunge. In many ways, grunge is the demon

flower grown from the bad seeds of punk, sown ten years earlier on European soil.

Before he was sixteen, Dave had joined up with a local band called Freak Baby. He was accepted after auditioning for guitar player. They played similar gigs to the earlier cover band he had been in, high schools and local halls, but now they were doing their own thing. The punk thing. They even recorded a demo tape in a four-track studio run by Barrett Jones. They ran off copies of the demo and distributed it themselves to some local record stores. They managed to gain a small local fan base made up of local skinheads. In America, the skinhead was the standard cut for fans of hardcore rock, politically-charged anarchic thrash, the USA's answer to punk.

Shortly after recording the demo, Freak Baby fell apart and reformed, minus the original bass player and with some instrument swapping. Dave Grohl conceded his

"We **want** to **reach** the Top **40.** Even if **the** whole of the **next** **album** can't get across to that type of **audience** there's at **least** a **hit** single or **two** in there."

Even before the line-up change, Kurt had been dissatisfied with the band, and its audiences.

guitar to take up drumming. The drummer — also a Dave — took up the vacant bass position. The new format was a vast improvement.

TO BE A SCREAMER

The band was renamed Mission Impossible. It was harder, faster and far more satisfying for all involved. The impossible mission lasted for about a year, but during that time they earned themselves quite a reputation as an accomplished hardcore band and were beginning to get live support slots for fairly major bands, such as Troublefunk. Ian Mackaye, of Fugazi, said good things about Mission Impossible. The only record released by

Say 'Big Cheese'. Several major labels wanted to get into grunge.

Mission Impossible was a shared double A-side with Lunchmeat, another local band who went on to become Girls Against Boys.

Grohl wasted little time and had soon pulled together another band called Dain Bramage. This was a threesome, with Grohl on drums, the other Dave from Mission Impossible on guitar and vocals and a new recruit, Reuben Radding, on bass. They became far more experimental than any previous band Grohl had been involved with. They found themselves playing local hardcore clubs, receiving a mixed reaction from the audiences, but attracting the attention of other musicians including Reed Mullin, drummer with COC, who gave them an introduction to Fartblossom records.

After favourable responses from their demo tape, once again recorded with Barrett Jones, Dain Bramage produced one album entitled *I Scream Not Coming Down*. The LP showcased their weird blend of traditional rock cliché and artcore punk. Grohl still believes it stands up for itself even today. Success was beckoning from the rocky horizons.

Again, the band was only to last about a year. Dave Grohl saw an advertisement: 'Scream looking for drummer — call Franz…'. Scream had been a favourite of Grohl's for many years and were well established and much respected. Scream had formed back in 1979 and Dave had learned some of his drum technique while playing along to their records. He phoned and got an audition lined up just because he thought it would be really cool to have the chance to jam with one of his favourite bands, not thinking he had a serious chance of getting through. When he turned up for the audition, instead of playing rock traditionals, Dave was able to play Scream drum tracks. The audition lasted two hours and, for an ecstatic Dave Grohl, was an achievement in itself.

He was invited back for a series of try-out sessions and eventually he realized he was in with a definite chance of joining Scream for real. Dave had to explain to Franz that he had not expected to get the opportunity, and already had a band, Dain Bramage, with his friends. They went their separate ways, but only for a few weeks. Dave went to see Scream play and was inspired by their magic. He contacted them right away and said he was theirs if they still wanted him.

THE ONE-MAN BAND

In the spring of 1987, Dave Grohl was drumming for Scream, one of DC's most respected rock outfits. They had recently moved record labels, from Dischord to another local label, Ras. Ras Records was primarily a reggae label that had chosen Scream to be the flagship band in its attempt to

Just going with the flow.

"The biggest guy I had ever seen and the scrawniest guy I had ever seen."

Monumental success looms with the new record deal pending.

crack the rock market. The band found themselves in a 24-track recording studio with a reggae producer to make the fourth Scream album, *No More Censorship*.

In February 1988, Scream took Dave Grohl on his first European rock tour. It was a rigorous two-month schedule spanning venues in Holland, France, Germany, Italy, Spain, Scandinavia and the UK. Owing a debt to the punk heritage of Europe, hardcore bands were welcome in Europe and Scream found themselves playing well-attended venues before enthusiastic audiences. Few of those venues were night clubs or concert halls. Mainly they were playing squats and student venues. Their show at Van Hall in Amsterdam was recorded and later released as a live album.

Between his commitments to Scream, Dave would help Barrett Jones out on personal projects and in return had extensive access to the eight-track in his basement. Dave discovered that he was able to play enough instruments well enough to record songs in a studio as a one-man band. He was able to knock out songs at quite a rate and began honing his writing ability. Some songs he had written and recorded himself in Jones's basement were adopted by Scream and used on *Fumble*.

Scream's final Euro tour was in the spring of 1990. They were booked to play twenty-three shows in twenty-four days! The strain began to take its toll and the line-up began changing. A gig in Germany was recorded as another line album.

On return from the tour, two members of the band, Pete Stahl and Skeeter, found themselves on the verge of eviction and so, with nowhere to live, took Scream back

Cigarette abuse can damage your feet: Kurt and Krist share that strange sense of humour again.

out on tour. Due to lack of planning, and virtually no advanced publicity, the tour was a disaster. They played to poorly attended venues, and on the night of a gig in Los Angeles, Skeeter, the bassist, went walkabout and could not be found.

The tour was put on hold while they tried to get a new bass player. It was around this time that Buzz Osbourne recommended Grohl to Nirvana and convinced him to fly up to Seattle for a try-out. He arrived at the airport with a huge carton containing his own drum kit, and a bag of clothes, to be met by Krist and Kurt. Dave still remembers this first meeting with Krist, 'The biggest guy I had ever seen and the scrawniest guy I had ever seen.'

SIGNED TO GEFFEN

On their return from Europe, Nirvana signed to Gold Mountain management, on the recommendation of Sonic Youth. Also around the close of the year, the single 'Sliver'/'Dive' was released through Tupelo in Europe and Kurt was reported to be rekindling the affair with his heroin. Kurt's personal life and relationship was a casualty of the recent stress that had publicly assaulted him. He broke up with Tracy Marander and moved out of their apartment in Olympia. Shortly after he took up with Tobi Vail of Bikini Kill for a short-lived and tumultuous relationship. After that pairing failed to take root, Kurt felt even more alone and inadequate and turned to drink and drugs for their faithful, though one-sided friendship.

Novoselic and Grohl felt shut out by Cobain and were worried about his increasing dependence on heroin. They were eager to begin work recording the next Nirvana album as they were aware the uncertainty would be detrimental to Kurt's state of mind. Nirvana had already agreed to sign with DGC, part of Geffen records, taking the advice of Sonic Youth, whom they all greatly admired. Only the contractual details needed to be finalized.

Sonic Youth were instrumental in Nirvana's signing to Geffen. (L-R) Lee Renaldo, Thurston Moore, Kim Gordon, Steve Shelley.

With the help of the new management team, contracts were soon in preparation with Geffen and in early January 1991 Nirvana were paid an advance of just over $287,000 (£185,000). This sum only just covered the band's debts, but this was more than made up for by a good royalties deal. While in limbo between labels, Kurt, Krist and Dave were almost broke and had to live frugally, biding their time before they could get into a recording studio again to record material for their new master, Geffen. It was reportedly on April 17, during this lull, that Nirvana first played a version of what was to be their massive breakthrough hit single, 'Smells Like Teen Spirit'.

'It upset me that we were attracting the people that a lot of my music. has a reaction against."

KURT COBAIN

Loner: Kurt shut out the others when the stress of a failed affair and early success-created tension.

A nice little story surrounds the writing of the song. Apparently, Kurt and a friend were talking about punk music and teenage rebellion. Later, after they had both got pretty drunk, Kurt found some graffiti on the wall. His friend had written 'Kurt smells like teen spirit'. Kurt took this to mean that he could be the person who sparked off teen rebellion and went away to write a song about teenage rebelliousness, how this is diffused with time, and the various ways that a punk rock star is perceived by an audience. Apparently, what the friend had really meant was that Kurt actually did smell of 'Teen Spirit'. There was a deodorant called 'Teen Spirit'... Kurt had not heard of the brand at that time.

Not quite off skid row: just before Nirvana made the big time.

Several renowned producers were suggested, such as Scott Litt, David Briggs and Don Dixon, but Nirvana were determined to work with Butch Vig again. Finally, all the contacts were signed and sealed by the end of April. Very soon after, Nirvana were able to start recording their Geffen debut album which would eventually be titled *Nevermind*. Butch Vig was brought in as producer at the Sound City Studios in Los Angeles.

TEEN SPIRIT VID

While recording the album, Kurt took time out to go to a Butthole Surfers gig at the LA Palladium, where he met a friend of David Grohl's, Courtney Love, who he had met at least once before. This time Kurt and Courtney seemed to click with each other and there were reports of them 'wrestling' on the floor.

Pittsburgh 1991

"So many **people think** it's the **epitome** of this **rebellious** high school **vibe.**"

DAVE GROHL ON THE TEEN SPIRIT VIDEO

By late June, *Nevermind* was nearly finished and needed one final mix. Butch Vig was unable to complete the final post-production, so Andy Wallace was brought in to add the finishing touches.

After the recording for the album had been completed, Dave Grohl took a few days off to work on a personal project he was developing. Around this time, Dave's good friend Barrett Jones had moved to Seattle and was sharing Dave's apartment as his roommate. With him, Barrett had brought his eight-track recording equipment.

He recorded a demo tape of material he had written, played and recorded by himself. He played the tape to Jenny Toomey of the Simple Machines record label who was impressed and asked if he would like to release a cassette through her label. Being so much in the limelight with Nirvana, Dave was a little hesitant but agreed to a small-scale release. The cassette was titled *Pocketwatch* and was given a limited release, copies being run off from a second generation version. *Pocketwatch* contained early versions of two songs, 'Winnebago' and 'Marigold', which were later to be used as Nirvana B-sides.

Nirvana, along with Sonic Youth, toured a selection of European summer festivals, making a massive impact at the UK Reading Rock Festival, where they placed alongside other US rock acts on the Friday. The Nirvana set ended in chaotic spectacle, with Kurt throwing himself onto and into the drum kit, dislocating his shoulder and surprising Dave Grohl, no doubt. That same day, Kurt and Courtney were seen talking. Courtney was at the festival with her then boyfriend, Billy Corgan of Smashing Pumpkins.

The video for 'Smells Like Teen Spirit' was made during August. The imagery of the video contained some almost biographical references. One of Kurt's first jobs was as a janitor, and here we see an older man with mop and bucket rocking to the groove that has passed him by — a could-have-been scenario. We also see the all-American cheerleaders giving it all they can before an audience of apathetic youths. The appeal of God and country and mom's apple pie never attracted Kurt...

Cobain was embarrassed by the size of the budget for the 'Smells Like Teen Spirit' video and would have preferred to have got some film student to do a more experimental promo for a fraction of the cost. But the video they ended up with was more than effective and was premiered on MTV in the popular *120 Minutes* show, the first time any band's debut video had managed to make it on to the show.

BATTERED GUITARS

Nirvana toured extensively during 1991, both in Europe and the USA. Around this time, Kurt was using a distinctive 1966 Fender Jaguar guitar. It was a 'tobacco-sunburst' colour pattern, with a red-swirl scratch guard, that had been customized so it had four knobs rather than the standard two. Two of these switches were always taped over to keep them set in position, and the original pick-ups had been replaced by what have been identified by some as DiMarzio Super Distortion pick-ups. He claimed to use piano wire for the top strings on his guitars, because guitar wire was neither thick nor tough enough for his style.

From the *Nevermind* promo photo sessions.

The sticker on the guitar reads: "VANDALISM: AS BEAUTIFUL AS A COP'S F..."

"I think **Bleach** is a **great** record, but there **was** a **very** fine line between **going** too **commercial** and keeping it **too** raw."

BUTCH VIG, BEFORE NEVERMIND

Nirvana break the surface...and sure make waves!

Another favoured guitar was a Fender Mustang in a light blue with a mother-of-pearl scratch guard. Kurt had said in interviews that the Fender Mustang was his favourite guitar. He mentioned a 1966 Mustang that he treated like a baby, and would not let anyone else touch it. Yet we see him regularly smashing and trashing guitars on stage... Observant members of the audience would have noted that often Kurt switched guitars for the final song of a live set. Sometimes it was an old Fender Stratocaster, but usually it was any guitar they could buy at junk shops during the tours.

Kurt used and abused a variety of guitars, some custom built.

If they had smashed their spare guitars and were unable to find cheap replacement guitars at local pawn shops, they would call Sub Pop HQ and get Jonathan Poneman to send them one by express courier. As Kurt played left-handed, these guitars would have to be re-strung, upside down.

Occasionally, fans would donate battered old guitars for them to smash up on stage at the end of the show. What had began as a gesture of frustration towards their audiences had now become part of the show and even involved audience participation! Kurt had, for a time, resented some elements that he saw in their audiences. He could see that their massive popularity was not only attracting people who shared his punk ethic, but also a

contingent of those who his lyrics actually attacked. As success increased, he became a little more philosophical about this: 'It upset me that we were attracting and entertaining the very people that a lot of my music was a reaction against. I've since become much better at accepting people for who they are. Regardless of who they were before they came to the show, I get a few hours to try and subvert the way they view the world. I would like to get rid of the homophobes, sexists and racists in our audience. I know they're out there and it really bothers me.'

WORKING THE PR MACHINE

The European tour ended in Rotterdam with another hard-rocking powerhouse performance...and Krist throwing a punch at the promoter for some unspecified reason. Shortly after, the milestone single, 'Smells Like Teen Spirit' was released on September 10, 1991. On September 20, Nirvana embarked on a major, six-week tour of the USA to promote the single and the album *Nevermind*, which was released by Geffen on September 24. Initial pressings for the LP were 40,000 of the US edition and 8,000 in the UK. It sold out within days of its release in both countries. Although some music journals had been raving about the band for some time, this instant crossover success was a surprise to the media and the record industry alike. Nirvana's breakthrough had been achieved without massive marketing campaigns and huge advertising budgets. Word of mouth, triggered by their live shows, was sufficient to ensure instant popularity at street level. Nirvana had become a phenomenon of the early Nineties.

Eventually Dave Geffen's record company realized that the potential they had hoped for was already more

than fulfilled and wasted little time in starting up the corporate push. With the grass roots success and respect already carrying Nirvana, the massive magazine and marketing campaign put sales of *Nevermind* above giants like U2, and the pre-scandal Michael Jackson. Nirvana's combination of success, across-the-board acceptability and credibility belittled cock-rock prima donnas Guns N' Roses, who had been Geffen's major cash cow until then. Kurt was not enamoured with the huge marketing ploy and hated pandering to the press right from the start. He admitted that he himself rarely read music journals and very rarely even looked at interviews with his favourite bands. He could only ever remember reading a couple of interviews with his faves, Butthole Surfers and the Pixies. He always stressed that the music was the main motivation for him and generally took the peripheral publicity with a grain of salt. He admitted that Geffen's band bio for Nirvana was mainly made up. Apparently the PR department had written up an accurate account of the band's roots, which came

Nirvana toured extensively throughout 1991 and on into 1992

Kurt was aware of how commercialization could trivialize.

Just after Nirvana made the big time.

across as 'really lame', so Nirvana wrote one themselves which ended up being a 'huge lie'. After all, in the entertainment industry an interesting lie is always better that a boring truth!

On October 12, *Nevermind* appeared at No. 144 in the US *Billboard* charts. On the night of that same day, after a show at the Cabaret Metro, Chicago, Kurt and Courtney Love were seen together at the after-gig party. Their behaviour was now obviously more than platonic, one report said that they appeared to be having sex against the bar! From this point onwards, Courtney Love was often present at shows during Nirvana's tour. Kurt and Courtney were usually seen together and it became clear that their developing relationship was more than casual. Courtney was later charged with assaulting Kurt's ex-girlfriend, Tobi Vail.

"I expected our core audience to buy our record within the first few weeks and that sales would decline after that. But after we were on MTV, I suspected we would sell a lot more."

KURT COBAIN

At the time, Courtney Love herself was becoming more of a name in the alternative rock scene than Kurt Cobain. Her band, Hole, had earned her quite a reputation throughout the USA and Europe.

THE BOARDING SCHOOL STRIPPER

Courtney was born Love Michelle Harrison on July 9, 1965. As a child she had been raised by hippies. Her father, Henry, had been in the hippy crowd hanging out with the Grateful Dead, gurus of Sixties rock. Her mother, Linda went on to become a therapist. Courtney was raised in New Zealand and Australia for much of her early childhood with her mother, before being sent to a boarding school in England. While back in Eugene, Oregon, USA, she lived with an analyst friend of her mother's. She was a dissatisfied, angry and rebellious teenager and was arrested for shoplifting (a Kiss T-shirt) and was sent to juvenile reform school, which she preferred to the boring boarding school.

After discovering the seminal music of Patti Smith, Courtney fell in with the new US punk scene and while back in the UK, she lived with Julian Cope of The Teardrop Explodes, becoming involved with the Liverpool-based post-punk new wave. Hole were later to reveal her early geographical influence when they covered a song by Echo & The Bunnymen.

Courtney went on to take any jobs she could land, including telesales, while becoming more and more enthusiastic to form her own band. She bought a guitar and began teaching herself to play. Her first stage experience was probably while working as a stripper in Alaska.

Courtney Love may have had confused emotions, as did Kurt. Like him, she expressed the conflict and confusion in lyrics, attitude and performance. From an early age

Hole in August 1991, when Kurt and Courney's relationship was in bud.

Courtney Love already had quite a reputation

Courtney was used to people around her taking drugs, but in those days it was LSD and pot. Now, as she found herself attracted to drugs in the rock subculture, the fashionable substance was smack. The many far more insidious forms of heroin were responsible for the fatalities of several close friends and lovers.

Back in Portland, Oregon, Courtney met a fellow stripper, Kat Bjelland and they began jamming together. They both moved to San Francisco, utilizing Courtney's trust fund to pursue their shared musical ambitions. Their first band was called Sugar Babylon, later changing name to Sugar Baby Doll. It featured Courtney, Jennifer Finch, later of L7, and Kat Bjelland who later went on to form Babes In Toyland. Courtney was, for a brief period, in Kat's

"It's about time **we don't** have to listen to **crap** on the **radio** anymore. Nirvana has **made** it possible for **bands** like **us** to have **constant bags** under our eyes from **all** the **hectic** touring. We **love them** for **that!"**

FER FINCH OF L7

band until the constant conflict of personalities forced her out. Courtney formed Hole in 1990 and also dabbled with a career as an actress, appearing in the Alex Cox movies, *Sid And Nancy* and *Straight To Hell*.

The video for Nirvana's 'Smells Like Teen Spirit' was put on the MTV regular playlist and sales of *Nevermind* went gold by October 29, 1991. Kurt's Nirvana stardom had surpassed Courtney's Hole in the space of a few months. They were soon to become known as America's premier punk couple.

L7's Jennifer Finch, who started her career in music with Courtney Love in the band Sugar Baby Doll recognized the impact of what Nirvana had done for other crossover bands, 'It's about time we can walk into a 7-Eleven and hear something cool. It's about time we don't have to listen to crap on the radio anymore. Nirvana has made it possible for bands like us to have constant bags under our eyes from all the hectic touring. We love them for that!'

Courtney was often present at Nirvana shows.

Nirvava never lost their punk ethic.

VANDALISM:
BEAUTIFUL AS A ROCK
IN A COP'S FACE
Courtesy of the Feederz: Office of Anti-Public Relations

A LITTLE HABIT

Nirvana were received like returning heroes at their Halloween homecoming gig at Seattle's Paramount on October 31. Kurt was aware even then that many of 'his public' would be thinking the band had sold out, signed to a major, playing bigger and bigger venues with increasing ticket prices. In interviews he was now giving on a regular basis to the music press he constantly denied this. It was really important to him that his audience understood that in corporate business there may have to be compromises but on an artistic level he would never lose his integrity. Nirvana would never lose its punk ethic, no matter how big they got, not while he had anything to do with it.

Dave Grohl was also concentrating on his own personal projects. He had Barrett Jones's eight-track at his disposal whenever he wanted to work. He concentrated on writing his own material during any time off he was able to grab from an increasingly hectic Nirvana schedule. Around this time he wrote and recorded versions of, among others, 'Alone And Easy Target' and 'Floaty', which were eventually to appear on his album *Foo Fighters*.

Kurt was beginning to resent both the scurrilous prying and blatant fawning of the music journalists. He admitted that he was already feeling like he was in a zoo, on display. He wanted the adoration and recognition from his audience in a narcissistic way, but did not have enough of the rock star ego to enjoy the increasing public scrutiny of his private self. He thought that he already gave enough of himself in his lyrics and wanted people to show more interest in the passion and playing of the songs rather than in the person behind them. He had always disliked the cult of personality. He genuinely lacked self-confidence on a personal, one-to-one level, and was very uncomfortable when people would expect him to be instantly wild and entertaining off the stage. He often thought that people treated him like a performing chimp. On occasions he tried to give them what they expected of him.

Kurt rocks out, doesn't sell-out.

Dave Grohl was working on his own projects.

Nirvana toured Europe through November and into December. The first and last dates being in the UK where their fan base had expanded – more like exploded – since their appearance at the Reading Rock Festival. The first date at Bristol's Bierkeller on November 3, was oversold and crammed with avid fans. During the entire tour, Kurt was said to have been suffering excessively from gastric flu, which aggravated his stomach problems. He self-medicated his own drugs, or used alcohol, to control the chronic pain. But there were lighter moments: 'I'd just like to say that Courtney Love of the pop group Hole is the best fuck in the world!' he proclaimed at the opening of their live appearance on UK Channel 4's late night TV show, *The Word*, on November 22. Hole were also touring Europe and Kurt and Courtney met up whenever their schedules coincided. In Amsterdam, they reportedly met and shared the drug experience of heroin together. A punkromantic gesture!

The single 'Smells Like Teen Spirit' was also released in November with the B-side carrying 'Drain You'. The

Having a smashing time!

December, 1991: Nirvana toured with the leading US breakthrough band, Red Hot Chili Peppers.

New Year 1992 saw Nirvana straight into another tour.

twelve-inch also had the tracks 'Even In His Youth' and 'Aneurysm'. Suddenly the disaffected youth of America and Europe had something that was fresh and distinctively their own. 'Smells Like Teen Spirit' became a new anthem for millions. The song was an attack on the apathy of the generation that now embraced it as their theme song. It vehemently criticizes the kind of angry teenager who is happy to be an armchair rebel. The type who use rock stars and punk icons to express, by proxy, what they feel themselves but are afraid to admit. It cajoled the majority of its audience.

    'Smells Like Teen Spirit' is the opening track on *Nevermind* and sets the tone for the entire album. 'In Bloom' again attacks elements of Nirvana's potential audience. Throughout his youth Kurt had been harassed and harangued by the local red-neck, logging, hunting and shooting contingent that made up most of his peers back in rainy Aberdeen. The song is a slag-off of the type of crass meathead who may hum along to the catchy riff on the radio while toting his gun and abusing anyone they perceive as weaker, more sensitive, more emotionally complete than themselves.

    'Come As You Are' explores the contradictions in what we say and what we think. How we act and how we think we should really act. What we may want opposed to what we really need. How the established social etiquette governs the way individuals comply, conform and consume, even against their own true will.

'Breed' attacks the class system and what it is like to be trapped in a white, middle-class, American upbringing along with all its conflicting values and morals.

    'Lithium' uses the analogy of a nervous breakdown of an individual to comment on the mass breakdown of society. Lithium for the patient, opium for the masses. Control of the symptoms rather than treatment of the cause.

    'Polly' is a completely deadpan account of the true events surrounding the kidnapping and repeated torture of a fourteen-year-old girl. Chilling in its portrayal of casual violence. Someone redirecting aggression away from the real cause of anger to a less intimidating, weaker target. Pointlessly abusing another in a futile attempt to vent frustrations. A physically stronger individual using another for purely selfish ends. The point of view expressed in the song is amoral rather than accusatory and caused some controversy because of this. Nirvana had, maybe mistakenly, given their audience a

Fashion is always a substitute for individuality, and here Kurt expresses his...individuality.

Utilizing feedback to achieve that distinctive Cobain sound.

LOAD UP ON DRUGS

'Drain You' is a song about sexual relationships and takes a Burroughsesque, almost clinical view of the subject. The song contains an interlude of throbbing drums, controlled feedback and slowly building guitar noise, a tip of the hat to the major influence of Sonic Youth.

'Lounge Act' is about how, sometimes, a personal aspiration is thwarted by a relationship. How it can be difficult to build a way of seeing without being smothered by another's.

'Stay Away', which was originally to be titled and include the lyric 'Pay To Play', confronts conformity and attacks people who form cliques to cover up their own inadequacies and fears.

'On A Plain' is a poetic attempt to express inexpressible emotions, to make tangible feelings that are hard to define.

'Something In The Way' deals with many aspects of loneliness, of being an outsider. It also contains a biographical episode based around the time Kurt spent living under the North Aberdeen Bridge as a youth, when he was homeless for a while.

'Endless, Nameless'— an unlisted bonus track — which was originally titled 'The Noise Jam', is probably the most experimental song on the album and developed out of a jamming session during the recording session for 'Lithium'.

By the end of the month, *Nevermind* was lodged firmly in US Top 10 album charts and the single, 'Smells Like Teen Spirit', was at No. 7 in the UK national chart. On November 28, Nirvana appeared live on the BBC's *Top Of The Pops*. Kurt altered the song subtly, singing it in a scary,

little credit for their intelligence and ability to think for themselves. Pointing rather than preaching is often far more effective.

The song was recorded using an acoustic guitar that Kurt had bought from a pawn shop for around $20 (£13). It was in such bad condition that it would not remain in tune for the duration of the song, hence the effectively atmospheric, but noticeably flat sound.

'Territorial Pissing' – like 'Mr Moustache' from *Bleach* – is an attack on the bull-headed macho male stereotype. Less than two years after Kurt's suicide, that same stereotype would be promoted and embraced by the culture called 'the new laddism', the retro-retard-rock music scene surrounding BritPop groups epitomized by Blur and Oasis.

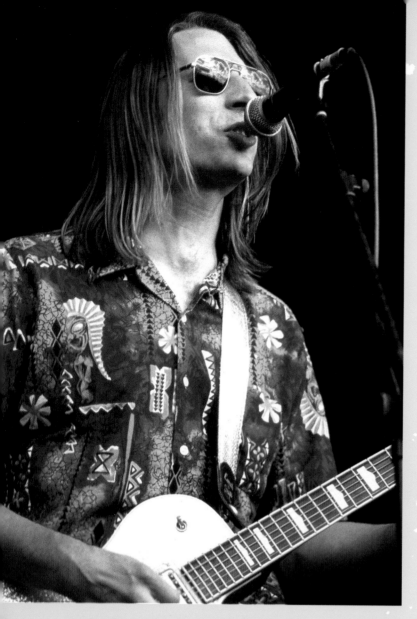

Mudhoney – the originators of grunge?

pseudo-psycho drawl and changing the opening line from 'Load up on guns and bring yr friends', to 'Load up on drugs and kill yr friends'. *Nevermind* sold over a million copies in six weeks, DGC had estimated total sales as 200,000.

The final date of the tour ended up at the Kilburn National in London on December 5. This concluded the tour prematurely, as the planned further dates in Scandinavia were cancelled. The gig ended with the equipment being hurled asunder, Kurt hacking into the stage with his guitar, Krist tossing his bass high, and Dave staggering around wearing the kick drum on his head... Again, replacement guitars were probably substituted for the last number trash-up jamboree.

They were flown from London back to the USA. Kurt and Courtney got together again when they both returned to Los Angeles, just before Christmas. They made no secret of their shared heroin habit among friends.

Success came so fast for Nirvana that they became superstars before they were given a chance to lose their street credibility. UK music paper *NME* called them 'The Guns N' Roses It's OK To Like'. The biggest rock band in the US and Europe had not had time to change their way of life. Krist was still driving a battered VW van and the band still rehearsed in a near derelict warehouse that they had been sharing with a commune of squatters who were growing marijuana in the basement.

Krist tried to sum up the surprise of sudden success: 'You enter a kind of identity crisis. You are a punk band with punk ideology, when suddenly you get into the mainstream. Are you different then all of a sudden?'

Mark Kates, the director of alternative music at Geffen commented, 'It was an amazing thing to be part of. No one even anticipated what happened – anyone who thought that a thing like this could even happen was full of shit.'

FRENCH KISSING IN THE USA

In the December of 1991, Nirvana did a short US tour with Pearl Jam and the Red Hot Chili Peppers. Shortly after this, the rumours of vehement rivalry between Kurt Cobain and Eddie Vedder of Pearl Jam began to crop up in the music press. It seems that Kurt did imply that Pearl Jam were trying to be rock stars by capitalizing on the hot Seattle scene, but there is little evidence to indicate any serious rivalry beyond the odd remark here and there, usually resulting from journalists continually comparing the two very different bands, just because they were both from Seattle.

The New Year 1992 saw Nirvana straight into another US tour. The tour was interrupted, on January 11, when they went to New York to take up an invitation to appear on the highly influential and hugely popular CBS show *Saturday Night Live*. Kurt and Krist caused a minor sensation among the twenty-five million viewers when they exchanged a full on French kiss for the cameras. *Nevermind* had been selling around three-hundred thousand copies a week, enough to knock Michael Jackson's *Dangerous* album out of the No. 1 slot in the US *Billboard* charts. Nirvana were already the flagship band of the new Seattle scene. They outsold and outshone all other successful Seattle contemporaries, such as Pearl Jam, Soundgarden, Alice In Chains and Mudhoney. The media was hooked on the new hype of what was now known as grunge. Kurt Cobain was aware that other Seattle bands were now being hauled onto their bandwagon by record labels already hungry for the next Nirvana, desperate to have a grunge band. He criticized Eddie Vedder and implied that his band, Pearl Jam, had sold out, changing their alternative approach into a parody of stadium cock rock metal in order to procure success. Kurt had been a friend of Vedder's back in the days he had known him in the earlier Sub Pop band Green River,

"It **was** an **amazing** thing to be **part** of. No **one** even **anticipated** what **happened** – **anyone** who **thought** that a thing like **this** could even **happen** was **full** of ●●●●."

Rick Boston of Low Pop Suicide, pioneers of the soft-heavy pop-punk sound now assocaited with Nirvana and the Seattle scene.

and although their rivalry was now to become quite public – and a little petty – it all eventually blew over and there was even talk of a joint project.

The term, 'grunge' was first seen in print as part of a strange but inventive marketing ploy by Mark Arm, who was responsible for bands like Green River and later Mudhoney. Apparently he advertised bands that did not exist and when their name was well and truly spread about, he or one of his cohorts, would write into music magazines criticizing the fictitious bands. One such letter contained the accusation that the band in question were 'Pure grunge!' It seems that the term was intended to be derogatory.

It is Bruce Pavit, of Sub Pop who is generally given credit with coining the phrase. In a press release accompanying a Green River release, the music is described as 'ultra loose grunge' and a later release for Mudhoney called their music, 'ultra sludge grungy glacial' among other things… Since that usage, grunge has been employed to describe the music of varied bands and musicians, from Kiss to Flipper, Neil Young to Sonic Youth.

Grunge was just a word, a label to define something that was difficult to pigeonhole in order to make it marketable. Stupidly, stores even began selling grunge fashions. Grunge and fashion should really have been self-cancelling phrases if used in the same sentence! As usual, though, money made its own rules and entirely missed the

Kurt often performed with stomach cramps brought on by the strain of touring.

Up on the roof – sales were going through it!

point. An image was marketed, but it was like selling a reflection – it looked similar but had no substance or soul. Fashion is always a substitute for individuality.

PREGNANT AND MARRIED

Kurt and Courtney moved into an apartment in Fairfax, LA. Shortly afterwards, Courtney discovered that she was pregnant and both she and Kurt promptly signed themselves into a detox clinic to kick their heroin addiction. Kurt and Courtney briefly considered a termination of the pregnancy, fearing the damage that their heroin habits may have done to the unborn foetus. After a series of tests, though, they

Kurt put on a brave stage face.

"I didn't think Nevermind would be **that** much different to Bleach – just a progression."

DAVE GROHL

Frances Farmer showing the strain after her arrest in 1943. Just one of the many victims of evil Senator McCarthy in the communist witch-hunt.

were satisfied that the baby was normal, and allowed themselves to recognize just how happy they were about being parents in the near future. This was immediately before Kurt left for a gruelling month-long tour of Australia, New Zealand and Japan. During the tour, Kurt's stomach pains became excruciating and he felt the need to score some heroin and use it. Instead he sought help and got some Methadone on prescription while in Australia.

As soon after the tour as possible, Kurt and Courtney were married in Waikiki, Hawaii, on February 24, 1992. This was the second attempt at marriage for Courtney, her previous time was short-lived and ended in an annulment. Dylan Carlson, a close friend of Kurt's from Seattle duo Earth, was Kurt's best man. The ceremony was very small and secret. Not even long-time friend and fellow Nirvana

colleague, Krist Novoselic and his wife Shelli, were invited. Kurt wore pyjamas and Courtney wore an old dress which used to belong to the actress Francis Farmer – a major role model for Courtney. The couple had allowed themselves to indulge their heroin habit immediately before the wedding to avoid the acute withdrawal pangs they were both suffering.

It's worth digressing to look at Frances Farmer more closely, since she was an important influence on both

Courtney and Kurt and became the subject of one of his songs. Farmer was a Hollywood actress and television hostess. Farmer would certainly have become extremely successful if it were not for interference from her delusional parents following a minor traffic offence which was blown out of proportion by an indignant judiciary.

Farmer was born in Seattle on September 19, 1914 and went to Hollywood as a young hopeful in 1936, after studying drama at Washington State University. Her good looks and talent helped her secure a seven-year contract with Paramount. She was young, energetic and wilful, not suitable characteristics for a lady in the depression years. Her parents were disturbed by her level of independence and the way she took charge of her own life, and so had her committed as mentally incompetent in 1942. This followed her arrest for driving with her lights on in a 'dim-out zone'. She had also been drinking and did not hold a current licence but exacerbated the whole situation by hurling abuse at the officer who had pulled her over. She was arrested and slammed in jail at Santa Monica.

REVENGE ON SEATTLE

Following a six-month sentence, Farmer was arrested for failing to show up for a parole report. She had recently broken up with her husband, Leif Ericson and had a messy affair with Clifford Odets which had caused her stress and heartbreak. Her frustration came to a head after her prison term when her behaviour became more outrageous. She had streaked topless down Sunset Strip and been involved in several brawls. The police came for her, once more, at her rooms in Hollywood's Knickerbocker Hotel. They smashed down her door and arrested her at gun point before cuffing her and dragging her naked through the hotel lobby.

"Everybody smokes during their pregnancy."

COURTNEY LOVE

As she was once again led into court she signed herself in as 'Frances Farmer, Occupation: Cocksucker'. As the judge read out her sentence, she called the gaggle of photographers 'rats' and then asked the judge, 'Have you ever had a broken heart?' before throwing an ink bottle at him. He denied her right to make a phone call and, as she was dragged away, she managed to knock a policeman to the floor and land a police woman with an effective punch.

Her mother came to Hollywood soon after these incidents, but instead of helping her daughter and providing support for her during this crisis, she eagerly signed commitment papers – and blamed communism for her daughter's nervous breakdown!

Frances was moved through a number of asylums for more than eleven years and was eventually released, after being given a lobotomy. After all this, she still went on to nurse her parents in their old age. The Nirvana song 'Frances Farmer Will Have Her Revenge On Seattle' is a fantasy about the revenge that she never took which was rightfully hers. Both Kurt and Courtney admired Farmer very much, maybe feeling something in common with her victimization – an empathy. Kurt had explained how he understood the situation that Farmer had found herself

Offstage, but not far from public scrutiny.
'I never realized that my private life
would be such an issue.'

May was cancelled. The three members of Nirvana had gone their separate ways for a while and it was too difficult to track each of them down and bring them together for the tour.

By this time Kurt's favourite left-handed Mustang was showing signs of wear. Kurt's playing style was pretty rough and ready and the instrument was threatening to fall apart. Kurt now realized that although good quality left-handed guitars were hard to come by he had the resources to have one built specially for him. He commissioned Danny Ferrington to make him a custom guitar based on the Fender Mustang design. It was very similar to Kurt's old Mustang but with an improved, Gibson-style bridge that keeps in tune longer under hard playing conditions. Also the neck was made straighter and stronger to withstand rough treatment. Kurt had faxed the specifications through and only saw the guitar when he came to pick it up. After playing a few bars, Kurt stated that it was his 'dream guitar'. Courtney, who was also there asked him if he would trash this one too, to which Kurt grimaced and emphatically stated that this would be his recording guitar. Undoubtedly, Ferrington must have been elated.

SUFFERING THE FALL-OUT

The planned tour of Europe for the summer of 1992 started with two dates in Ireland. The morning after Nirvana played Belfast, Kurt collapsed and required medical attention. A statement made to the press suggested that the rigours of travelling and too much junk food had irritated a stomach ulcer. It turned out that the cause of Kurt's collapse was methadone withdrawal.

During the following Euro dates, Nirvana were dogged by reports in the press of infighting, fall-outs and tantrums. It seems that all the fury was set off by Kurt insisting that

trapped in: 'I realize how and why such things can happen. How it even can happen to me, if you don't recognize certain mechanisms in time. Luckily, nowadays it's not that easy any more to plan something like that. That McCarthy period was so paranoid; every form of strange behaviour was recognized as a symptom of communism. I hope nobody will experience something like Frances did. Did you know that people who were in on that scheme still live carefree in Seattle? I can work myself into a lather by thinking about that. If I had the means, I would bomb their houses flat!'

The single 'Come As You Are' was released in March, but the promotional tour scheduled for April and his royalty share be increased for all Nirvana material from Nevermind from then onwards. Courtney has been blamed by many for this change in attitude, but it is just as likely that the couple wanted more money for their forthcoming family. Maybe Kurt, being the creative dynamo behind Nirvana and principal writer for nearly all the songs, felt that his declining level of enjoyment needed compensating in some way to make a continued career worthwhile.

Kurt was genuinely worried about the state of Nirvana and his relationship with his two colleagues. He was, by all accounts a very thoughtful and generally 'nice' guy. All the arguments and friction seriously affected him – he felt responsible for making sure

"I **knew** that when I had a **child**, I'd be **overwhelmed** and it's **true**... I can't **tell** you **how** much my **attitude** has **changed** since we've got **Frances**. **Holding** my **baby** is the **best** **drug** in the **world**."

KURT COBAIN

The proud and happy parents, Courtney and Kurt with baby Frances Bean.

Grunge baby.

Into the eyes of the media hurricane.

everyone got what they wanted, Krist and Dave, their audience, Courtney and his child to be.

Back home, on August 4, Kurt checked into Cedars-Sinai clinic for more detox treatment. Allegedly, he had by then worked his heroin addiction up to a £250-a-day habit. The controversial, and now notorious, article by Lynn Hirschberg in that month's issue of *Vanity Fair* magazine implied that Courtney was still regularly using heroin while pregnant. It seems that there was little or no evidence to support these accusations. The photo of a pregnant Courtney that accompanied the feature was doctored to remove the cigarette that she was smoking. Tobacco can be harmful to unborn children, but is not perceived as being in the same league as heroin.

With the vindictive elements of the press sensationalizing the claims made in the *Vanity Fair* article and creating a media storm around Kurt and Courtney, their healthy daughter, Frances Bean, was born safe and sound on August 19, 1992, also at the Cedars hospital. Contrary to common belief, Frances was not named after Frances Farmer, but in honour of a friend of the Cobains, Frances McKee, a member of the The Vaselines. When asked about Frances Bean's name, Kurt has said he wished he had thought of naming her after Farmer, and explains that the name Bean is from the pet name he and Courtney called their daughter after a sonic scan showed her as a cute bean shape. A careful examination of the 'Lithium' single cover reveals that the seemingly abstract picture on the left side is, in fact, a reproduction of that sonogram.

Almost immediately, the LA Department of Children's Services began their unsuccessful campaign, based primarily on the allegations in *Vanity Fair*, to investigate the couple and take their baby away from them. For a while Courtney's sister, Jamie, took care of young Frances while

the law suits were thrown back and forth. Courtney filed charges and tried to sue a nurse she claimed had leaked her medical records. The music press lapped it all up, but the notoriously right-wing mainstream press of the USA and UK really tried to portray the Cobains as losers, abusers and generally low-life no-hopers. The establishment always tries to destroy or control any non-conformist elements that become successful and popular.

DRUGS: A WASTE OF TIME

By August 30, Kurt was out of detox and Nirvana were the Sunday headlining act at UK's Reading Rock Festival. Kurt was brought onto the stage in a wheelchair, wearing a hospital theatre smock. It was the same smock he wore at his daughter's birth.

In interviews around this period, Kurt was inevitably asked about drugs and about being a father. He answered, 'I knew that when I had a child, I'd be overwhelmed and it's true... I can't tell you how much my attitude has changed since we've got Frances. Holding my baby is the best drug in the world.'

Expounding on the subjects of using drugs and becoming a possible role model, Kurt was always quick to destroy the glamorous image often attached to junkie rock stars, saying, 'I chose to do drugs. I don't feel sorry for myself at all, but have nothing good to say about them. They are a total waste of time.'

Returning from Europe, Nirvana appeared on the MTV Awards show, September 5. Standing at the podium, accepting the Best Newcomer award, Kurt addressed the

camera and the millions watching, 'It's really hard to believe everything you read.' He was, of course, referring to the recent articles attacking both his and Courtney's personal life and drug addictions. He once commented that 'If I had known about all this crap, I would've thought twice about putting myself in the public eye so much. I had no idea people could abuse you so much.'

They had planned to showcase the track 'Rape Me', but pressure from the MTV studio directors dissuaded them and they agreed to play 'Lithium' instead. When Nirvana took to the stage for the live broadcast, they taunted the MTV officials by playing the opening bars of 'Rape Me' before changing tack and performing 'Lithium' as promised. They won two awards.

Kurt and Axl Rose from Guns N' Roses reportedly came near to blows backstage at the awards ceremony. Animosity had been developing between Kurt and Axl for some time. Axl had asked Nirvana to support Guns N' Roses on one of their tours; they declined. Axl also requested that Nirvana play at his thirtieth birthday celebrations; Kurt turned him down again. Apparently, while Kurt, Courtney and Frances were eating in the diner, Axl walked past and Courtney called him over. On the spur of the moment, Kurt asked Axl if he would be Frances's godfather. Axl flew off the handle and reportedly shouted abuse at Kurt saying, 'You shut your bitch up or I'm taking you down to the pavement.'

'Everyone around us just burst out into tears of laughter,' Kurt later recounted to *The Advocate*, 'She wasn't even saying anything mean, y'know. So I turned to Courtney and said "Shut up, bitch!" And everyone laughed and he left. I guess I did what he wanted me to do: be a man.'

SMASH IT UP

Kurt has since been openly critical of the music of Geffen label-mates Guns N' Roses calling them 'pathetic and untalented'. He went on to say, 'I used to think that

Live and very alive. Playing music was Kurt's motivation and reward.

> **"I chose to do drugs. I don't feel sorry for myself at all, but have nothing good to say about them. They are a total waste of time."**
>
> KURT COBAIN

Nirvana's second Reading Rock Festival: in just one year they had rocketed from cult status to cultural icons.

everything in the mainstream pop world was crap. But now some underground bands have been signed with majors, I take Guns N' Roses as more of an offence. They're really talentless people, and they write crap music, and they're the most popular rock band on the earth… I can't believe it!'

Kurt was pleased to be part of school yard rivalry between Nirvana fans and Guns N' Roses fans, 'It's really cool. I'm really proud to be a part of that, because when I was in high school, I dressed like a punk rocker and people would scream "Devo!" at me – because Devo infiltrated the

mainstream. Out of all the bands who came from the underground and actually made it in the mainstream, Devo is the most subversive and challenging of all. They're just awesome. I love them.'

Nirvana took time out from their own busy schedule to do a surprise appearance as special support guests for Mudhoney. They used this opportunity to showcase material from their forthcoming *Incesticide* album. Some of the songs were so old that Kurt had forgotten the original lyrics and was making up new ones on the spot. No one noticed or minded.

At the end of the set, Matt Lukin, bass player with Mudhoney, brought two children onto the stage. The gleeful expressions on the eight-year-old faces turned to nervous

NAKED EMPATHY

William S. Burroughs, born in 1914, is the literary outlaw responsible for among others the notorious *Naked Lunch* and *Junky*, and is arguably one of the most important authors of the twentieth century – whether you like his work or not. His infamous trial for obscenity, and his acquittal, has ensured freedom of speech in literature more than any campaign or legislation could have. Burroughs's entire lifestyle has been on the periphery of social acceptability, often meandering in and out of the criminal realms. He shot and killed his wife (accidentally, he claimed) while doing a 'William Tell party trick' down in Mexico. He is openly bisexual with homosexual preferences both in his writing and behaviour, and acted so openly, even when homosexuality was illegal throughout the USA. He has been a drug addict and wrote freely and honestly about the subject. His books and behaviour made him an exile in Paris, London and Tangiers, for most of his life.

Burroughs has been cited as an influence for many artists and rock groups from Duran Duran ('The Wild Boys') to Coil. He is credited with first coining the term 'Heavy Metal'. In recent years, because of his stature as a modern cultural icon, he has gained a recognition deserved for decades. He appeared with Matt Dillon in the movie *Drug Store Cowboy*, and was played by Peter Weller in the semi-biographical film of *Naked Lunch*.

The influence of Burroughs can be clearly seen in the structure of many of Cobain's lyrics, and sometimes in their content, especially in the *Nevermind* track 'Drain You'. In fact, literary figures had been almost as important an influence on Kurt's writing as his rock heroes and heroines. His favourite book was *Perfume* by Patrick Suskind, but he had long been a great admirer of Burroughs's works. It was an empathy with the wry, often scathing humour as well as its darker side. And the dark side was on the rise.

apprehension as they suddenly realized they were in front of a huge hall packed with thousands of strangers. Krist offered one of the kids his bass, the child was obviously thrilled, as was the other when he found himself with Kurt's guitar slung around his shoulders. They both bashed away on the strings, encouraged by the indulgent crowd who started chanting 'Smash it up! Smash it up!' The kid with the bass was suddenly possessed by the spirit of rock and made a brave, but ineffective, attempt to break up the guitar. This had to be done by the experts...

In an interview in the *LA Times*, September 21, Kurt admitted that he had 'a little habit', when asked about his unwanted image as a drug addict. Shortly after, in October, he was working with one of his greatest heroes and hard-drug exponent, William S. Burroughs. Kurt provided the atmospheric guitar landscape that acts as backdrop for Burroughs's distinctive drawl as he reads, *The Priest They Called Him*. The ten-minute collaborative track was released the following year on CD and ten-inch vinyl formats. The ten-inch was a single-sided disc with the autographs of Kurt Cobain and William S. Burroughs etched into the other side.

Reading: Kurt in bimbo wig and hospital smock.

Kurt: pensive as Reading rocks.

LOVE IS TOUGH

During October, Kurt and Courtney both left threatening massages on the telephone answering machines of Britt Collins and Victoria Clarke, who were planning to write a dirt-dishing exposé on Nirvana. Kurt was already sick and tired of the way that the media hounded him and Courtney. 'The biggest thing that affected me,' he had said, 'was all the insane rumours, the heroin rumours...all this speculation going on. I felt totally violated. I never realized that my private life would be such an issue.'

Following the video's MTV push, the single 'In Bloom' came out just ahead of the December 15 release of the album, *Incesticide*. *Incesticide* was a mixed bag of tracks including four dating back to the original Nirvana demo of January 1988. Other tracks were out-takes from the *Nevermind* recording sessions and some taken from sessions recorded for BBC sessions. It was more like a collection of rarities aimed at the true fan, rather than a follow-up to *Nevermind*. It lacked the cohesion of a true album and was probably released to capitalize on the band's meteoric success. Nirvana had just started preparation for their proper follow-up album and had enlisted famed guitar abuser and ex-Big Black, Steve Albini, as the producer.

In January 1993, Nirvana played a couple of big gigs in Brazil. Nirvana were trying to avoid any long tours now. Kurt's stomach condition, which appeared to have symptoms similar to an ulcer but remained undiagnosed, could not tolerate the stresses and dietary trauma of extended touring. He was attending pain management classes and learning to meditate. It was his stomach condition that had originally lead him into developing a heroin habit, in order to numb the pain. He blamed the symptoms of his stomach trouble, for initiating most of the rumours in the press that he was a wasted junkie. Journalists would come backstage to do interviews and Kurt would be crouching, holding his guts, looking agonized, or vomiting, or generally being distracted because he was fighting nausea while giving interviews.

In interviews, Kurt expressed his satisfaction with what Nirvana had achieved.

Krist posed for the cover photo for the Cobain/Burroughs collaboration, 'The Priest They Called Him', but is most at home with his bass.

The single 'Oh The Guilt' was released by Touch & Go Records, a double A-side, shared by 'Puss' performed by The Jesus Lizard.

On February 14, Nirvana began recording their next LP with Steve Albini. They had booked the recording studio under the moniker of The Simon Ritchie Group. During March, Kurt and Courtney moved into a house on the banks of Lake Washington, and the LA Department of Children's Services failed to take possession of Frances Bean when their entire case against the Cobains' suitability as parents was thrown out of court. Kurt and Courtney were obviously relieved and elated. Kurt was quoted as saying, 'I don't even care about

the band as much as I used to. I know that sounds shitty, but the band used to be the only thing that was important to me in my life, and now, I have a wife and a child. I still love the band, but it isn't the only thing I'm living for.'

Dave Grohl continued pursuing his own projects and recorded more songs that would later become *Foo Fighters* material, including 'For All The Cows' and 'Weenie Beenie'. He was also having fun recording cover versions of some of his favourite tracks. He did a version of ex-Kiss Ace Frehley's 'Ozone' and 'Gas Chamber', originally by irreverent US hardcore pioneers Angry Samoans. Grohl approached an independent record label based in Detroit with a view to releasing some of this material. He hoped to remain anonymous and mainly wanted to release the songs so he would have a decent recording to send to friends.

A relaxed moment: Krist shares a thought.

After an absence from US live gigs for more than six months, Nirvana played a special benefit show in aid of Bosnian rape victims in San Francisco on April 9, 1993. To some this gesture was a surprise as Nirvana had not been perceived as a political band. Krist Novoselic probably felt strongest about their motivations for doing the show. He explained, 'Although you don't find it in the music, it doesn't mean Nirvana is no political band. We are very concerned with things happening everywhere. I am of Croatian origin myself, so how could the events over there have no effect on me? If we have discussions between ourselves, it's almost always about politics. That has never been different. We were raised in Reagan's period – a very frustrating period. Via groups like MDC [Millions Of Dead Cops] I discovered punk rock, and contextually that was always about politics. Unadapted behaviour, that was the heart of it. That's what infected us. And that's still in us...'

After notorious New York noise merchant Steve Albini had finished mixing the new album, Kurt called in another producer, Scott Litt, to remix the tracks 'All Apologies' and 'Heart Shaped Box', the track with most potential as single releases. Albini was disgruntled by this and in an interview for *Entertainment Weekly* he accused the band of selling out. Kurt Cobain obviously took umbrage at Albini's remarks and wrote a letter to *Newsweek* magazine in which he explained that, 'Being commercial or anti-commercial is not what makes a good rock record. It's the songs. And until we have the songs recorded the way we want them, Nirvana will not release this record.'

Rumoured titles for the forthcoming album included *Verse Chorus Verse* and *I Hate Myself And I want To Die*. By the end of April, Nirvana had confirmed that the title would actually be *In Utero*.

GUNS N' POSES

On May 2, Kurt was treated for a heroin overdose at Harborview Medical Center in Seattle. He was still convinced that his habit was not an addiction and Courtney initiated a campaign of 'Tough Love'. The so called tough love 'treatment' is based on a rather dodgy, and generally dubious, psychological method of changing detrimental behaviour patterns in an individual. A potentially destructive pattern is supposedly disrupted when everyone who is close to the individual withdraws their help and support, effectively shunning an individual who is, by definition, in need of help. The idea is that when someone is confronted with losing everything that is really important to them, they realize the error of their ways and seek help to change. The major premise that is used to justify the method is that the effect of self-will has a more powerful and permanent effect than the advice of others.

On June 4, the police were called to the Cobain household after a row when Kurt attempted to throttle

Kurt hugs his aching belly.

"The **biggest thing** that affected me **was** all the insane **heroin rumours.** All this speculation **going** on. I felt **totally violated.** I never realized **that** my **private** life would be **such** an **issue.**"

KURT COBAIN

Candid Kurt.

Courtney, after she had thrown fruit juice in his face. The police presence settled the matter, and three guns were removed from the premises. All the confiscated weapons were later returned. At the time Courtney told reporters that the argument was over the presence of the firearms in their home. Courtney thought them unnecessary, Kurt wanted them. He told one interviewer that he was not the hippie people liked to think he was. Apparently, when he received a really bad or vindictive write-up, he would buy a gun or some ammunition and mentally carve the responsible journalist's name on it. Other sources, predictably, blamed the row on Kurt's heroin addiction.

Nirvana made a surprise appearance at the New Music Seminar in New York City on July 23. This event was doubly

> **"Although you don't find it in the music, it doesn't mean Nirvana is no political band. We are very concerned with things happening everywhere. If we have discussions between ourselves, it's almost always about politics."**
>
> **KRIST NOVOSELIC**

surprising, because on that morning Kurt had overdosed on heroin and may well have died if it had not been for Courtney's intervention. She recognized the symptoms immediately and acted quickly, using a strictly controlled, possibly illegal, drug to counteract the heroin. The drug is thought to have been buprenorphine, which is an opiate that adheres to the same neuro-receptors used by other opiates, such as heroin, thus blocking their effect. Some sources suggest that Kurt's collapse was not due to an overdose, but to 'cotton fever'. Cotton fever is a condition suffered by people who take drugs intravenously, without taking enough care during preparation. Addicts often use cigarette filters or cotton wool to strain the solution before injecting. Occasionally, tiny filaments of the cotton fibre are taken up into the syringe and enter the blood stream. When these tiny clumps of fibre block blood flow they can cause extreme pain and serious cramps. Either way, buprenorphine would be effective, either as an analgesic or a heroin blocker. Kurt performed with Nirvana that evening and showed no evidence of his near brush with death.

REVEALING THE WOMB

The first single, 'Heart Shaped Box', from the new album was released in August, and Nirvana embarked on their first US tour for two years. For part of the tour they recruited John Duncan, of Goodbye Mr Mackenzie, as a second guitarist to fill out the live sound. Later, Duncan left to fulfil commitments with his own band and Nirvana added Pat Smear as second guitarist, who had formerly been with LA punkers The Germs. During the tour, at a gig in Hollywood on September 8, Kurt was joined by Courtney on stage for the first time.

During the Michael Lavine photo sessions for the *In Utero* sleeve and publicity material, Kurt was reported to

Nirvana played a gig in aid of Bosnian rape victims, April 1993. 'I am of Croatian origin myself, so how could the events over there not affect me? —Krist.

84

Good, clean-living lads.

have been high, smacked out and uncooperative. This was probably true, but he may have also been unhappy or tired after touring and doing the rounds of press interviews.

In one such interview, Dave Grohl commented on the forthcoming album with accurate insight: 'We think *In Utero* will get three types of reactions. For the listener-by-accident, spoiled by *Nevermind*, this album sounds like our commercial suicide; probably he-she will ignore it, and consider us "one-hit wonders". The sceptics will rate it a pretentious album: "Nirvana makes some noise and think they are good at it." The fans, finally, will instinctively like it. They will rate the album at its true value: a spontaneously realized, no-nonsense album, without the post-production polish.'

In Utero was released on September 13, 1993. It was not what many fans had expected, some were disappointed, some where in awe of its brilliance. Kurt had implied prior to its release that it would be a harder, punkier outing than their previous work. It was not. Factions of the music press had predicted a more commercial, pop offering. It was not. It turned out to be a real rarity: a mature rock album. Although the production values evident on the record were rougher than *Nevermind*, the melodies were well structured, veering away from their previous soft-hard formula. The lyrics were deeply personal and lovingly crafted.

In addition to the photos taken by Michael Lavine, the sleeve also carried liner notes which included the statement, 'If any of you in any way hate homosexuals, people of different color, or women, please do this one favor for us – leave us the fuck alone! Don't come to our shows and don't buy our records.' Apparently, this angry notice was included in response to some nauseating reports of a rape that took place in Reno in 1991, when two men sexually assaulted a woman while chanting a Nirvana song.

There was almost no post-editing involved on the majority of the songs. Most of the album was recorded in one take, as if it were a live set up, with very little over-dubbing or studio trickery. *In Utero* emerged as an honest recording of

"I don't **even** care **about** the band as much as I **used** to...the **band used** to be the **only** thing that was **important** to **me** in my life... now **I** have a **wife** and a **child** the **band** isn't the only **thing** I'm **living** for."

KURT COBAIN

87

the group. There were a few little cracks and creaks that may have been taken out by some producers, but left in lend the whole thing some genuine character. Nirvana knew that they had not conformed to the commercial formula, they hoped that they would not gain any new mainstream fans with this LP. Things had got so big that it was all a little out of hand. To some extent, they hoped that this honest album would sort out the real fans who understood the band's ethic from the bovine element of their audience who just like to sing along vacuously to their catchy little ditties.

IGNORANCE IS BLISS

Dave Grohl summed it up when he pointed out that, 'The pressure is on the record company, not us. They have to sell the album. We just went into the studio and recorded what we liked and no one meddled with that. Then we mixed everything, gave the master tape to Geffen and said "this is it". It's up to them to make the link to the mainstream. I just think this time it will be harder to do that, because if you work with Steve Albini – he has some pretty obstinate production standards – you know you won't get a radio-friendly sound.'

When they went into the studio, only half of the compositions were ready. The rest developed from improvization in the studio. With the self-imposed restrictions of a two-week deadline and a limited recording budget, the whole creative process remained immediate and focused.

'Serve The Servants' is clearly autobiographical, recounting and summing up the experience of being in a band fraught with the stresses of success. 'Scentless

Kurt proclaims his early influences: Flipper are one of the genuine US hardcore bands.

Apprentice' was based on the novel *Perfume* by Patrick Suskind. 'Heart Shaped Box' has a simple lyric which manages to convey complex themes of love and entrapment. It certainly deals with aspects of his relationship with Courtney and his addictions to her and heroin. 'Rape Me' is a simple story song, it tells a tale of poetic justice when a rapist is put in prison for his crimes and is then raped there himself.

'Frances Farmer Will Have Her Revenge On Seattle' is another story song, inspired by Frances Farmer and the injustices she suffered at the hands of McCarthy's America and her own parents. 'Dumb' is a drug-themed song which basically draws the conclusion that 'ignorance is bliss'. 'Very Ape' is another treatment of a favourite subject: attacking the macho male in all its stereotypical splendour

In Utero tour, 1993. Angels approaching.

"If **any** of you hate **homosexuals**, **people** of different **color**, or **women**, please **do** this one **favor** for us – leave us **alone!** Don't **come** to **our shows** and don't **buy** our **records."**

LINER NOTES FOR IN UTERO

The angelic Kurt Cobain

Nirvana tried to avoid lengthy tours...'Dynamite comes in small packages.'

of stupidity. 'Milk It' can be seen as a kind of sequel to 'Drain You' and again uses very Burroughsesque clinical terms to examine co-dependency. Kurt traces the origin of this clinical approach to description to his chronic stomach illness. 'I tend to think those medical associations have to do with a stomach condition that I had for years which only recently disappeared. My mother had the same thing when she was my age. It lasted for five years and then it was suddenly gone. I've read a lot of medical manuals and had discussions with people who have chronic stomach aches, because I wanted to know what I had. In the long run it all became a bit obsessive, and probably led to the textual basis for the new album.'

'Pennyroyal Tea' is about abortion, the dilemmas and difficult issues surrounding the subject, the arguments for

and against, the inevitable guilt that will follow. 'Radio Friendly Unit Shifter' is a basically meaningless conglomeration of poetic ideas meant as a skit of record industry marketing techniques, particularly the corrupt 'plugger' system used to get radioplay for singles.

'Tourette's' takes its name from the syndrome which causes sufferers to move jerkily and shout, spit, or swear spontaneously and without control. Kurt shouts and screams quite a bit on this one. 'All Apologies' is dedicated to Courtney and Frances, and the lyrics seem pretty obscure, probably meaning more to the two people it was meant for than to all the other listeners put together.

THE GUITAR ENDORSER

Nirvana were awarded the Best Alternative Video award at the MTV Video Awards. Later that year, in November, the withdrawn track 'I Hate Myself And I Want To Die', also a preliminary album title, appeared on the compilation album, *The Beavis & Butt-head Experience*.

The second *In Utero* single, 'All Apologies', was released on December 6, 1993. Just over a week later, the *Nirvana Unplugged* sessions, recorded on November 13, were

Toronto, 1993.

Favourite grunge pullover.

broadcast on MTV on December 16. This session was later released as an album and also on video. It was an assured performance, musically sublime, with Kurt delivering the lyrics in a strangely poignant manner, his face almost angelic in its calmness.

Later that month Nirvana were the headlining act on MTV's New Year's Eve special. Here we saw Kurt with

**One of the world's biggest rock acts,
Nirvana at the height of the stardom.**

Roseland, NYC, July 1993.

what appeared to be another, new custom guitar. It was a
modified, sonic-blue Fender incorporating some features
from both the Jaguar and the Mustang. Kurt later
commissioned a special Jag-stang custom from the Fender
Custom Shop. He presented them with a composite photo
of his ideal guitar. He had taken a photo of a Jaguar and a
Mustang, cut them in half and joined them up to create a
hybrid – this was the design he gave to the makers. Fender
produced a prototype and sent it to Kurt. He tried it out
and wrote his suggestions for alterations on the guitar
before sending it back. After the few alterations and
adaptations were made he had a guitar perfect for his
distinctive style.

The Jag-stang custom had a body that was a merging
of the two guitars and a Mustang-style, short-scale neck.

Kurt was entirely satisfied with the finished product and was
offered a possible endorsement if the design went into
production as Fender now intended. He said that, 'Ever since
I started playing, I've always liked certain things about
certain guitars but could never find the perfect mix of
everything I was looking for. The Jag-stang is the closest
thing I know. And I like the idea of having a quality
instrument on the market with no preconceived notions
attached. In a way, it's perfect for me to attach my name to
the Jag-stang, in that I'm the anti-guitar hero – I can barely
play the things myself.' Kurt had turned down an offered
Gibson endorsement because he was unable to find a Gibson
model he liked.

The next year, 1994, was to be a telling period for
Nirvana. They were by then one of the world's biggest rock
acts. They were announced as the headliners for the
potentially huge Lollapalooza 4 tour. Even though *In Utero*
had not been as well received as it might, it had
consolidated their status, and tickets for Nirvana's first UK
tour since 1991 sold out entirely on the morning of
February 2, as soon as they became available.

"**I** **don't** want to **play** the rock'n'roll pundit... I'm just a **bass** **player** in a band. I **don't** think **any** of us **feels** qualified to **be** a spokesperson for a **generation.**"

KRIST NOVOSELIC

Backstage at the MTV awards, Krist with Chris Cornell of Soundgarden.

LA Forum, December 1993

A MISREPORTED DEATH

In interviews of this period, Kurt expressed his satisfaction with what Nirvana had achieved as a band, but there was also an element of doubt about the future creeping in. 'I don't know how long we can continue as Nirvana without a radical shift in direction.' He stated, 'I have lots of ideas and ambitions that have nothing to do with the mass conception of grunge that has been force-fed to the record buying public for the last few years. Whether I will be able to do everything I want to do as a part of Nirvana remains to be seen. To be

97

"The **quality** is xxxx, **and** you find **these** things **selling** for a **fortune** in the **record** shops."

**Could've been or should've been?
Eddie Vedder fronts Pearl Jam.**

fair, I also know that both Krist and Dave have musical ideas that may not work in the context of Nirvana. We're all tired of being labelled. You can't imagine how stifling it is.'

During the night of night of March 3, Kurt collapsed in Rome after an adverse reaction to mixing champagne with the drug Rohypnol. He was admitted to hospital the next morning under the assumed name of Kurt Poupon and by lunch time, news that Kurt Cobain was in irreversible coma was spreading throughout the news media. These reports turned out to be wholly inaccurate. He remained in coma for twenty hours. It was reported as an attempted suicide – he had apparently swallowed more than sixty of the tranquillizer pills.

**1994 was to be a telling, and
ultimately tragic, period for Nirvana.**

At about this time Courtney Love was interviewed by *Select* magazine and made some remarks which in context were examples of her irreverent wit, but now take on chilling irony. Commenting on the inaccurate reports that Kurt was dead, she said that she would have hated being Yoko. She also said that she wished it had been Eddie Vedder who was in the coma, commenting that they would 'have a fucking candle-lit vigil for him'. She also denied

99

that Kurt had attempted suicide, claiming that the overdose was accidental, even though it happened after they had a tiff. Later, the LA Times was to report that a suicide note had been found in their hotel room.

As soon as he became coherent, Kurt wrote a brief message on a pad at his bedside: 'Get these fucking tubes out of my nose.' When the tubes were removed and he was able to speak, his first request was for a milkshake, strawberry flavour. Some reports claimed his first words on waking were 'Fuck you,' but it is not clear to whom these were directed, or why. A press statement from Nirvana's PR office stated that Kurt had suffered a 'complete collapse due to fatigue and severe influenza' and that he had 'combined prescription pain killers with alcohol'. On March 8, he was

discharged from hospital and went into retreat with Courtney and Frances.

A portent of things to come: On March 18, police were once again called to the Cobain home. Courtney had made the call after Kurt had locked himself in a room with a gun and had been threatening to shoot himself. The police entered the premises and confiscated twenty-five boxes of ammunition and four guns: three pistols and a semi-automatic rifle – the same guns that they had taken away the previous June, plus an extra one. This time they were not to be returned. A bottle of pills were also taken away to be tested.

GOOD SHOTGUN ADVICE

Rumours were now rife that the Cobain marriage was in jeopardy, and there may well have been some truth in those rumours. Courtney has since admitted that, in retrospect, their relationship was heading towards destruction of one sort or another. We will never know how much truth was

Daddy's little girl.

embodied by the many rumours. We do know that some of those rumours were malicious lies and journalistic fabrications. It is difficult for an outside observer to assess any relationship. Many couples who do not, on the surface, seem compatible are completely happy and well matched. The view from within that each of those people has of the other may be very different to what someone else perceives. Also, just because a relationship does get into difficulties or break up, that does not diminish the depth and intensity of feelings experienced prior to its demise. Who said love has got to last forever?

Tom Grant, a private investigator who claims to have been hired by Courtney to find and follow Kurt, has stated that Courtney had already started divorce proceedings by this time. He also put forward a plethora of other allegations and accusations which he claimed to have proof to back up. So far, no proof for any of his serious allegations has been presented to anyone, anywhere.

After the cancellation of European tour dates, a revised tour schedule was announced on March 26 and a statement was made to the press that Kurt was 'restored to full health'.

Kurt was said to be showing the strain of success, but seemed fairly happy and stable to those around him. He was worried about the security of his home and family and on or around March 30, he met with his friend Dylan Carlson, who had been his best man at the wedding. Kurt asked Dylan to purchase a shotgun on his behalf because Dylan was a gun enthusiast and would know what was the best weapon for the purpose. Also, Kurt was worried that if he had bought the gun in his own name, the police may have confiscated it due to the recent problems he had experienced with them. Dylan believed that Kurt genuinely wanted the gun for home protection and did not think Kurt seemed depressed or suicidal. He reportedly took Kurt to Stan's Gun Shop in Lake City Way, to the north of Seattle, and bought a used 20-gauge shotgun for about £200. Carlson said that Kurt seemed apprehensive about the pending rehabilitation treatment he was signing up for, but was generally optimistic and not despondent.

"Whether I will be able to do everything I want to do as a part of Nirvana remains to be seen. We're all tired of being labelled. You can't imagine how stifling it is."

KURT COBAIN

NEVER FADE AWAY

Kurt checked into the Exodus Recovery Center, a small facility for drug rehabilitation based at Daniel Freeman Memorial Hospital in Marina Del Rey, California. He did this after being convinced by Courtney due to an 'intervention'. Intervention is a term used to describe a hard-hitting and confrontational therapy in which a drug addict is made to face up to, and attempt to justify, their habit. Close friends talk to the addict and confront them with evidence to break down their denial. In this case the close friends were Dave Grohl, Krist Novoselic and representatives from Nirvana's label management, along with some family members.

He only lasted two days at the clinic, spent sharing a room with Gibby Haynes of the Butthole Surfers, before discharging himself. During the two days he spent at the clinic he spoke over the phone to Courtney to

Kurt Cobain – alive, but not well in Paris. One of the last photos of Kurt onstage, 1994.

congratulate her on Hole's new album, *Live Through This*, he told her that he loved her and asked about Frances. He did not say that he would be leaving or tell her where he intended to go.

Kurt's mother filed a missing persons report with the Seattle police on April 2. It was very unusual for Kurt to disappear without telling anyone where he was. Since disappearing, he had not contacted Courtney, who was in LA at the time, undergoing treatment for withdrawal from tranquillizers. Police checked out his known haunts and visited the couple's house, but failed to find Kurt.

On the evening of Monday, April 5, 1994, Kurt Cobain put the loaded 20-gauge shotgun to his head and pulled the trigger. That was how his world ended – not with a whimper, but with a very loud bang. The tortured spirit of Cobain had abruptly left its suffering vessel, blasting off into the nether void. Oneness with the Absolute. Kurt did not hear that gunshot, but a few days later, it resounded loud and clear throughout the media. Its ricochet still rings in the ears of millions today...

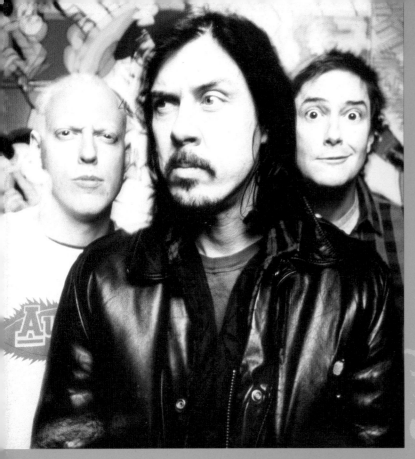

Butthole Surfers – one of Kurt's all time faves. Gibby, front and centre, was rooming with Kurt and was one of the last people to see him alive.

It has since been reported that Kurt had phoned a friend to ask how someone could most efficiently kill themselves with a gun. The friend had, apparently, thought that this information was research for a song lyric, as Kurt's tone of voice and manner had seemed normal.

Cobain's corpse was discovered on Friday morning, April 8, by an electrician who first reported his find to the press and then to the police. The shotgun had been loaded with light-load shot, the kind recommended for home protection. It will not penetrate walls, and spreads wider at close range, giving even the worst marksman a chance of hitting a target. At point-blank range it is just as effective as any. Kurt had left an ID card with a photo of himself on the floor next to him, as if he knew that this would be the only way to recognize him immediately after the event. He was later officially identified by his fingerprints.

Although anyone who commits suicide must be in a very desperate and unsound state of mind, Kurt had taken the time to write a heart-rending and eloquent note.

"Because we were stupid enough to do drugs at one brief time, we realize that we opened ourselves up to gossip by people in the rock world. We never dreamed it would be reported as if it were true."

COURTNEY LOVE

In this he described his emotional state and gave some explanation as to his motives, but there were obviously many factors involved in bringing him to the conclusion he reached with such finality. There has been much conjecture, character smearing, idolizing, accusing and theorizing surrounding the events leading up to Cobain's death. There were even rumours of foul play, accusations of murder.

Cobain had always been emotionally fragile and over sensitive – this is partly why his heartfelt lyrics struck a chord in so many others. He carried a burden of frustration and anger, towards the world, towards others, towards himself. He also had a great deal of love for the world of others, but not, it seems, for himself.

He had been using hard drugs, on and off, for many years and had overdosed many times, sometimes nearly fatally. His use of drugs stemmed from self-medication to alleviate chronic stomach pains and back trouble.

The warning signs were clearly there to see, even in his lyrics; after all, had he not written: 'I Hate Myself And I Want To Die'? As with Ian Curtis of Joy Division before him, the management and record companies were blinkered by dollar signs. They welcomed the constant publicity. Close friends were caught up in the same meteoric success. Fans identified with his lyrics of tortured alienation... They all missed the point, but sadly, Kurt Cobain did not.

Courtney Love had been concerned about Cobain's state of mind immediately prior to the suicide and had even hired investigators to track him down. It seems that while a few people were searching for Kurt, he was lying dead in the conservatory, or 'greenhouse', at their home. The gunshot was still hanging in the air, waiting to be heard by the world.

I NEED TO BE NUMB

At Kurt's memorial service Courtney read extracts from the suicide note. In the note Kurt explained that he had lost all enthusiasm for creativity, saying, 'I haven't felt the excitement of listening to as well as creating music, along

The 'greenhouse' behind the Cobains' home – scene of the suicide.

with really writing something, for too many years now... I need to be slightly numb in order to regain the enthusiasm I once had as a child...'

He quoted two lines from the Neil Young song 'Hey, Hey, My, My (Into The Black)': 'It's better to burn out, Than to fade away.' He also apologized to his fans for not appreciating his stardom enough and implied that to go on would be faking it and betraying them. This could be seen as a sensitive poet buckling under the pressure of money-driven corporate contracts. *Nevermind* – the record that catapulted Nirvana to super stardom – is one of the all-time great classics of rock. *In Utero* would have been hailed as a breakthrough masterpiece if any other band had put it out. Instead, it was perceived by many as a weak and pale sister

The body formerly occupied by Kurt Cobain is removed from the scene.

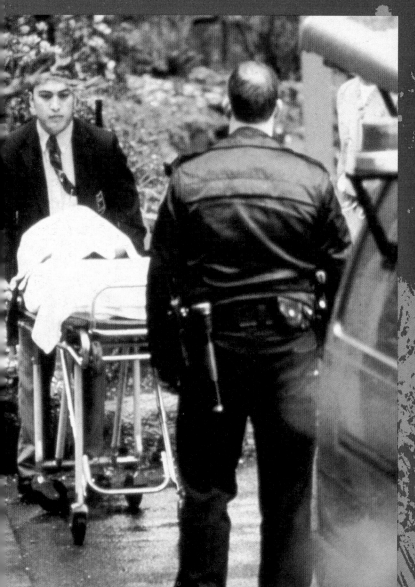

"I **haven't** felt the **excitement** of **listening** to as well as **creating** music, along with really writing something, for too many years now... I need to **be slightly numb** in order to **regain** the enthusiasm I once had as a **child...**"

KURT COBAIN

in comparison to *Nevermind*, made up of tracks that Kurt was obviously not happy with. Maybe in retrospect he was not happy with his achievement, but at the time it had been the record that Nirvana wanted to make. It would have been better for Kurt to take time out and sort his problems before writing another record, but the corporate machine runs off cash and respects only sales, not the individuals that make those sales possible. Record labels all too often fail to appreciate that creativity is a most valuable resource and sometimes needs to be nurtured not exploited. Geffen were perhaps a little more understanding than most: they could not have predicted the huge success of Nirvana and so could not presume to dictate how the band's music should develop. Nirvana were left well alone while recording their material and Geffen only stepped in when it came to marketing.

Somehow, even the saddest, most unfortunate tragedy can be glamorized by the rock industry. Kurt Cobain has already been elevated to legend status and is used as a kind of yardstick against which the sincerity of a musician's angst can be measured. To be held in the same esteem as Cobain as a tortured poet, do you have to kill yourself? What is overlooked is that Cobain was a very troubled individual, and nothing positive resulted from his suicide.

Fans mourn Kurt Cobain at Seattle's Center Pavilion.

If he was still alive, his songs would be no less potent and effective, only there might be more of them.

MTV set up a telephone help-line to counsel distraught fans.

On the following Sunday evening, April 10, Kurt was remembered and mourned at two ceremonies in Seattle. A public vigil, organized by the office of Seattle's Mayor, Norman Rice, was held by the light of hundreds of candles at Seattle's Center Pavilion. Around five thousand fans and admirers were present to share a heartfelt tribute to the late prima poet of US punk.

Across the city at the Unity Church Of Truth, on Eighth Avenue, near the famous Denny Park, a private memorial service was held for around two hundred of Kurt Cobain's close friends and family. There was no casket or urn at the ceremony, just people united in their mourning. All details of Kurt's cremation have been kept from the media. This secrecy ensures that Kurt Cobain is able to rest in peace and not become another tourist attraction like Jim Morrison's grave.

107

THE UNFAIR SPLIT

The memorial service was presided over by a Reverend Stephen Towles, who read Psalm 23 before giving a brief speech in which he said: 'Kurt's life has affected millions – and not many people can say that.' Although suicide is counted as a sin by the Christian Church, Towles made a point of dispelling this attitude, likening the feelings and emotions to having a finger jammed in a tightening vice: 'The pain becomes so great that you can't bear it any longer'. He then asked those present to close their eyes and

Fans unite in their grief: the memorial vigil at Seattle's Center Pavilion.

"**Kurt's** life has affected **millions**— and **not** many **people** can say that. What word **describes** him? **What** did he **mean** to you? Was there anything left **unsaid?** **Touch** him..."

REVEREND STEPHEN TOWLES

Joy Division's Ian Curtis preceeded Kurt by some years— he hanged himself

reflect on Kurt's life. He asked everyone, 'What word describes him? What did he mean to you? Was there anything left unsaid?...Touch him...'

Immediately after, several friends and associates of the Cobains addressed the mourners. Krist Novoselic said of Kurt: 'His heart was his receiver and his transmitter... That's the level that Kurt spoke to us on, in our hearts – that's where he and the music will be always be, forever.' He urged everyone: 'Remember Kurt for what he was – caring, generous and sweet. Let's keep the music with us, we'll have it forever.'

Bruce Pavitt, of Sub Pop records, expressed his love and respect for Kurt, though he was saddened that he had been, 'a few days late in expressing it'.

Courtney, welcoming support from her long-term friend and cohort, Kat Bjelland, struggled to retain some composure. Courtney spoke for some time. She read passages from some of Kurt's favourite poems and books and from the Bible as well as extracts form the suicide note. She also recounted some poignant anecdotes about his life, including his childhood when he had an imaginary friend.

Kurt and Courtney's personal manager, Danny Goldberg asked Kurt to 'send a few messages to us once in a while – you got us hooked... it's unfair to split like this.' He then went on to share some words of consolation with the grieving widow saying, 'I believe he would have left this world several years ago if he hadn't met Courtney.' These words of support must have provided prophetic comfort to Courtney in the months to come when the world's media and music press would all but accuse her of being the main instrument in Kurt's death.

Tapes of some of the private memorial service speeches were later played at the public vigil, as well as a special message Courtney had recorded for her fellow mourners. In it she read from Kurt's suicide note, commenting on it all the while with bitter and emotional humour. She had recorded the message while lying in the bed that she and Kurt had shared at their home. The massive crowd sat in silence as Courtney's tearful and emotional voice echoed through the hearts of a generation.

IN MEMORIAM

Courtney: *'I don't know what to say... I feel the same way you guys do. If you guys don't think... to sit in this room where he played guitar and sang, and feel so honoured to be near him, you're crazy... Anyway, he left a note – it's more like a letter to the fucking editor – I*

The lifestyle of Jim Morrison of the Doors was his own suicide. Courtney did not want Kurt's grave to be a tourist attraction or shrine like Morrison's had become.

"His **heart** was his **receiver** and his **transmitter**... **That's** the level that **Kurt** spoke to **us** on, in **our hearts** – that's **where** he and **the music** will be **always** be, **forever.**"

don't know what happened, I mean it was gonna happen, but it could've happened when he was forty. He always said he was gonna outlive everybody and be a hundred and twenty...

'I'm not gonna read you all the note cos it's none of the rest of your fucking business. But some of it is to you. I don't really think it takes away his dignity to read this considering it's addressed to most of you. He's such an asshole! I want all of you to say "asshole" really loud...

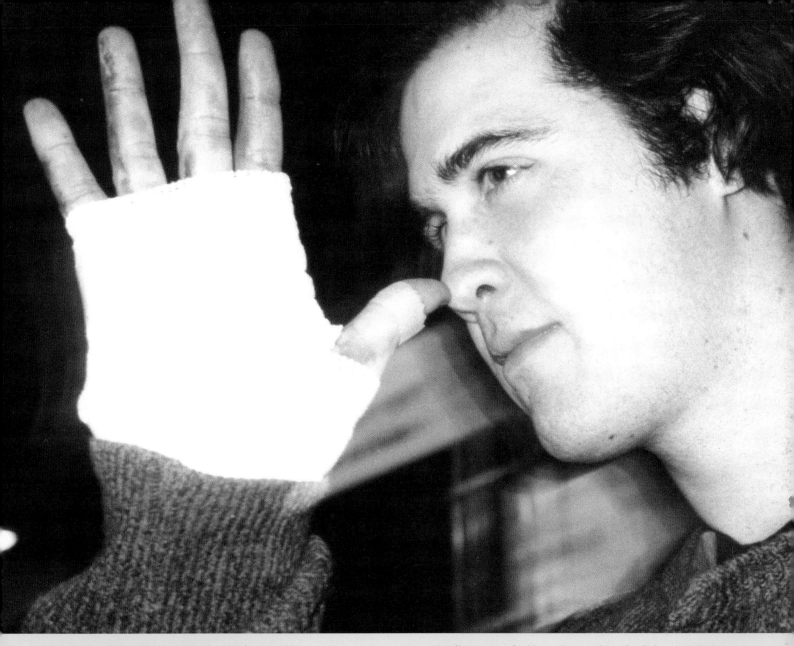

Krist Novoselic spoke at Kurt's service. Now he devotes himself to worthy purposes and is not as often in the limelight.

' "This note should be pretty easy to understand. All the warnings from the punk rock 101 courses over the years since my first introduction to the, shall we say, ethics involved with independence and embracement of your community, it's proven to be very true...

' "I haven't felt the excitement of listening to as well as creating music, along with really writing something, far too many years now.

' "I feel guilty beyond words about these things – for example, when we're backstage and the lights go out and the roar of the crowd begins, it doesn't affect me the way in which it did for Freddie Mercury, who seemed to love and relish the love and adoration of the crowd..."

'Well Kurt, so fucking what – then don't be a rock star, you asshole!

' "...which is something I totally admire and envy. The fact that I can't fool you, any one of you, it simply isn't fair to you or to me. The worst crime I could think of would be to pull people off by faking it, pretending as if I'm having one hundred per cent fun..."

'Well, Kurt, the worst crime I can think of is for you to just continue being a rock star when you fucking hate it, just fucking stop!

' "Sometimes, I feel as I should have a punch-in time-clock before I walk out onstage. I've tried everything within my power to appreciate it, and I do, God believe me I do, but it's not enough. I appreciate the fact that I and we have affected and entertained a lot of people. I must be one of those narcissists who only appreciate things when they're alone. I'm too sensitive. I need to be slightly numb

in order to regain the enthusiasm I once had as a child. On our last three tours. I've had a much better appreciation of all the people I know personally, and as fans of our music, but I still can't get out the frustration to gather the empathy I have for everybody. There's good in all of us and I simply love people too much."

'So why didn't you just fucking stay?

' "So much that it makes me feel just too fucking sad. Sad little sensitive, unappreciative pieces…"

'Jesus man! Oh shut up, bastard! Why didn't you just enjoy it? I don't know… Then he goes on to say personal things to me that are none of your damn business – personal things to Frances that are none or your damn business…'

Although Kurt Cobain's lyrics had explicitly dealt with alienation and frustration, it is the final paragraph of his suicide note that finally brings home the depth of feeling that he was struggling to get across to others. Courtney concluded her distressing reading of the note:

' "I had a good marriage, and for that I'm grateful. But since the age of seven, I've become hateful toward all humans in general, only because it seems so easy for people to get along that have empathy. Only because I love and feel for people too much, I guess. Thank you all, from the pit of my burning, nauseous stomach for your letters of concern during the last years. I'm pretty much of an erratic, moody person and I don't have the passion any more. So remember, it's better to burn out than fade away. Peace, Love, Empathy-Kurt Cobain."

'And then there is some more personal things that is none of your damn business… and just remember, this is all bullshit… And I'm laying in our bed, and I'm really sorry, and I feel the same way you do. I'm really sorry you guys-I don't know what I could have done. I wish I'd been here. I wish I hadn't listened to other people, but I did.

'Every night I've been sleeping with his mother, and I wake up in the morning and think it's him because his body's sort of the same… I have to go now…'

"The **worst crime** I could think of **would** be to **pull** people off **by faking** it, pretending as if I'm **having** one **hundred** per cent **fun**…"

KURT COBAIN

Rock'n'Roll samurai: Henry Rollins had toured with Nirvana and was no stranger to the deaths of close friends.

The tape, which had been recorded the night before, was destroyed after it had been played.

NOT THE WHY BUT THE HOW AND WHEN

The site of the public vigil was littered with photographs of Kurt, balloons, inflated condoms and the ashes of burnt garments. Emotions had run high, fans had moshed in the fountains to Nirvana songs played over the PA. Police were present throughout, but there was little need for them; two people were cautioned and one arrested for suspicion of assault.

The music of Nirvana had affected millions. Those millions now felt the effect of this tragic loss. A few were not strong enough to stand the buffeting from the shock waves of Kurt's suicide and chose to join him. Daniel Kasper, a Seattle local, was the first fan to kill himself. Kasper was already depressed for several reasons, and Cobain's death had been the final straw. He also died of a self-inflicted gun shot. A Seattle crisis centre reported more than twice as many distressed callers than usual, a situation similarly reflected in New York when the Samaritans received double the normal amount of calls. A wave of copycat suicides among the nation's youth was feared.

The death of Kurt Cobain will continue to be examined and considered by many. There will always be conjecture and apportioning of blame. The truth, of course, is that no one will ever know the whole story, no one will ever entirely understand the reasons why. The answers died with Kurt.

The Seattle police conducted a special investigation into the circumstances surrounding Kurt's death. They were careful to be seen to be thorough, and were endeavouring to clarify several important points. What was the exact time of death? The County Medical Examiner had determined the time of death to have been sometime on April 5, yet the police had two people who claimed to have spoken to Kurt on April 6.

Why was the body undiscovered until April 8? Kurt's mother had reported him missing on April 2, and there were other people looking for him, as well as workmen at the house where his body was.

They wanted to find out if there was any connection between Kurt's disappearance and Courtney's reported overdose on April 7. Was there any truth to the rumours that Courtney had left Kurt?

Where was Courtney at the time? Geffen had issued a statement claiming that she was in London on April 8, while LA police reported that she was in Beverly Hills. The latter turned out to be true – she had not travelled to London as expected.

Was there any truth to the rumours that Nirvana had in fact split up?

There was evidence in the house that Kurt had spent the evening preceding his suicide with a mystery visitor… this person's identity remains unestablished.

ONLY THE BACK CATALOGUE

Geffen mourned the passing of Kurt Cobain… Nirvana were no more. After the initial surge of record sales immediately following his death, there would be only the back catalogue. Without Kurt, Nirvana could not continue. There would be a hole in the lives of millions of fans.

Of course, the tragedy on the personal level overshadowed any commercial considerations. Hole's latest album, ironically titled *Live Through This*, was pushed into stage-centre and now Courtney, no stranger to controversy and journalistic assassination attempts, had to contend with increasing accusations, bad-mouthing and back-stabbing. Much of this was brought on herself through her abrasive and careless manner while under public scrutiny over past years. She could take it in her stride before, now she had to handle it while still dealing with her consuming grief. Friends from the music world came forward to lend their support. Michael Stipe from R.E.M., whom Kurt had planned to work with, was there to console and comfort the widow. Henry Rollins, also a friend of the Cobains and no stranger to the deaths of close friends, also tried to ease Courtney's grief.

The denied rumours that Courtney had been having an affair with Evan Dando from the Lemonheads were fuelled when the photos of her and Evan in bed together were printed shortly after Kurt's death. Tom Grant, the private investigator submitted a report implying that Kurt's death was not suicide but in fact murder. His report and allegations have been closely examined by the police and by a multitude of interested

"Since the age of seven, I've become hateful toward all humans in general. I'm pretty much of an erratic, moody person and I don't have the passion any more. So remember, it's better to burn out than fade away."

KURT COBAIN

"I don't **think** any of us **would** be here if **it** were **not** for **Kurt Cobain.**"

DAVE GROHL

Dave Grohl has picked up his career with new group, the Foo Fighters.

parties via various electronic media worldwide. Nothing had been found to support any of his outrageously conspiratorial claims.

Neil Young was shocked at the loss of Kurt Cobain and said he would never again be able to play his song, 'Hey, Hey, My, My' because it was now too painful. He has since been persuaded to reintroduce the song into his live shows as a memorial to Kurt. Pearl Jam performed a cover version of the Neil Young classic within a week of Kurt's death, but they omitted the lines that he had quoted in his suicide note. Eddie Vedder, who for so long had been painted in the music press as Kurt's arch-rival, told his audience, 'I don't think any of us in this room would be here tonight if not for Kurt Cobain.'

FOO FIGHTERS

Krist Novoselic has become more active in environmental campaigning since the end of Nirvana, and has also built a reputation as a political spokesperson for his native Croatia and the plight of its people. Because he is serving a worthy purpose, which nonetheless lacks the glamour and appeal of the rock world, Krist is not as often in the limelight as his colleagues.

Dave Grohl has since recorded an album of his own compositions under the name of the Foo Fighters. After Kurt's death, Dave had felt lost and no longer had the will to continue making music. He was wondering what to do with his life when he received a letter from fellow Seattle band 7 Year Bitch. They too had recently lost one of their members and realized just how Dave must have felt. The note said: 'We know what you're going through. The desire to play music is gone for now, but it will return.'

Dave decided to do what he had always wanted and booked himself a twenty-four-track studio for a week. He went in with his stash of about forty songs and picked the ones he felt the most comfortable with. Barrett Jones helped out as producer, but the only other musician to be involved was Greg Dulli, lead singer and principal songwriter with The Afghan Whigs. Dulli played guitar on the track 'X-Static'. The recordings were all done in that one week and Dave had a hundred copies duplicated to hand out to friends and record company representatives. That tape became one of the most pirated recordings of the year. Dave described it as spreading 'like the ebola virus'.

After recording the songs, Dave then decided he needed to put together a band. This was definitely an unconventional way to go about forming a new group! He sent a tape to Pat Smear, who he knew from previously working with him for the 1993 Nirvana live shows. Smear expressed great interest in signing up for the new band and joined on lead guitar and backing vocals. In mid 1994, another Seattle-based band, Sunny Day Real Estate, who had released one album on Sub Pop, broke up. Grohl had witnessed a couple of their final shows and had been blown away by the musicianship. Both Nate Mendel and William Goldsmith from the band signed up to join Dave Grohl and Pat Smear. Dave found himself working with a band once more, with Nate on bass and William on drums.

They called themselves the Foo Fighters, the name taken from the strange lights seen in the skies by pilots in World War II, also known as Kraut Balls. (Foo Fighters were seen by US Air Force pilots flying missions over Germany and parts of France towards the end of the war. Theories were put forward that they were some new and secret German weapon, as they were known to cause radar interference and faults in electrical instrumentation. These strange lights, which moved in an odd, unnatural manner, remain unidentified flying objects to this day. Reports during the latter months of the war became so frequent that it was forbidden to report them and they were explained away as the natural electro-static phenomenon, St Elmo's Fire.)

NO BURN-OUT

More recently there have been plans for several Nirvana tribute albums. An advert appeared in Seattle music periodical *The Rocket* for any bands 'inspired by Kurt's life/death' to get in touch as potential contributors to a project titled *Requiem For Kurt Cobain*. Another album, simply titled *Tribute*, was to feature original compositions by contemporary bands, mainly Seattle-based, including Frank Cox from the city's Love Mongers, Mission Impossible and Artis The Spoonman.

And so it ends. And so it will continue. The legacy and legend of Nirvana...

Their music touched millions and their influence is still resounding around the world. Nirvana made it possible for many bands that would otherwise have remained in the underground to break through. They changed the face of popular music. While across the world, the effect of punk was becoming diffused by techno-dance music and middle-of-the-road, easy listening, standard rock, Nirvana swept across the barriers of genre and smudged the boundaries between the categories of compartmentalized pop pap. They made people listen with open hearts and encouraged the new wave of bands to play using theirs. Music was important again.

Nirvana did not burn out, and they will not fade away...

DISCOGRAPHY

Song titles are listed as printed on the package. Figures in parenthesis for CD track listings are duration in minutes and seconds. Kurt Cobain plays guitar and vocals, Krist Novoselic plays bass on all tracks unless stated otherwise. Krist Novoselic listed as Chris Novoselic before in Utero. Kurt Cobain has also been spelled as Kurdt Kobain. has also been spelled as Kurdt Kobain. Nirvana tracks have also been included on numerous compilation albums.

LINE-UP (VARIATIONS)

Kurt Cobain: vocals, guitar (1985-1994)
Krist (Chris) Novoselic (1985-1994)
Aaron Burckhard (1985-1986)
Dale Crover: drums (1988)
Chad Channing (1986-1990)
Jason Everman: guitar (1989)
Dave Foster: drums (1988)
Dan Peters: drums (1990)
Dave Grohl: drums, backing vocals (1990-1994)
John Duncan: guitar (1993)
Pat Smear: guitar (1993-1994)

ALBUMS

BLEACH
1989:

LP on Sub Pop (SP34,US)
LP on Waterfront (DAMP114, Australia)
Released in June. First 1,000 copies pressed on white vinyl.

Next 2,000 copies included a free poster.
LP on Tupelo (TUPLP6, UK)
Released in August 1989. First 300 copies pressed on white vinyl, necxt 2,000 copies pressed on green vinyl.

TRACKS: Blew, Floyd The Barber, About A Girl, School, Big Cheese, Paper Cuts, Negative Creep, Scoff, Swap Meet, Mr. Moustache, Sifting

CS on Sub Pop (SP34a, US)

TRACKS: Blew, Floyd The Barber, About A Girl, School, Love Buzz, Paper Cuts, Negative Creep, Scoff, Swap Meet, Mr. Moustache, Sifting, Big Cheese
CD on Sub Pop (SP34b, US)
CD on Tupelo (TUPCD6, UK)

TRACKS (42:43): Blew (2:53), Floyd The Barber (2:15), About A Girl (2:46), School (2:40), Love Buzz (3:33), Paper Cuts (4:04), Negative Creep (2:52), Scoff (4:07), Swap Meet (3:00), Mr. Moustache (3:21), Sifting (5:21), Big Cheese (3:40), Downer (1:42)

April 1992
CD ON GEFFEN (US)
TRACKS: as above but re-mastered

CREDITS: All tracks written by Kurt Cobain, except for 'Love Buzz' written by Robby Van Leeuwen (Shocking Blue). Dale Crover plays drums on 'Floyd The Barber', 'Paper Cuts' and

'Downer'. Chad Channing plays drums on all other tracks. Recorded in Seattle at Reciprocal Recording by Jack Endino, December 24-29, 1988. Front cover photo by Tracy Marander. Inner photo by Charles Peterson. Design by Lisa Orth. Execution by Jane Higgins.

NEVERMIND
1991

LP on DGC (DGC-24425, US)
CS on DGC (DGCC-24425, US)
CD on DGC (DGCD-24425, US)

TRACKS: (42:36): Smells Like Teen Spirit (5:01), In Bloom (4:14), Come As You Are (3:38), Breed (3:03), Lithium (3:15), Polly (2:54), Territorial Pissings (2:22), Drain You (3:44), Lounge Act (2:36), Stay Away (3:31), On A Plain (3:14), Something In The Way (3:51)

CS on DGC (DGCC-24425, US)
CD on DGC (DGCD-24425, US)

TRACKS: (59:23) Smells Like Teen Spirit (5:01), In Bloom (4:14), Come As You Are (3:38), Breed (3:03), Lithium (4:15), Polly (2:54), Territorial Pissings (2:22), Drain You (3:44), Lounge Act (2:36), Stay Away (3:31), On A Plain (3:14), Something In The Way...Endless, Nameless (20:36)

CREDITS: Released on September 24, 1991. 'Endless, Nameless' is an unlisted track which appears ten minutes after the end of 'Something In The Way'. (This track was accidentally omitted from initial US pressings, and from all foreign pressings.) All tracks written by Kurt Cobain and Nirvana. 'Territorial Pissings' begins with a short excerpt from Youngbloods 'Get Together', written by Chet Powers. Dave Grohl plays drums on all tracks. Kirk Canning plays cello on 'Something In The Way'. Produced and engineered by Butch Vig and Nirvana. Mixed by Andy Wallace. Recorded May-June 1991, at Sound City Studios in Van Nuys, California. Cover photo by Kirk Weddle. Inner photos by Michael Levine. Monkey photo by Kurdt Kobain.

NEVERMIND, IT'S AN INTERVIEW
1992

CD promo on DGC (DGC CD-PRO-4382, US)

TRACKS: (53:44)
Track 1: Breed, Stay Away, School, Mr Moustache, Sifting, In Bloom, Spank Thru, Floyd the Barber, Scoff, Love Buzz, About A Girl [live, full], Dive, Sliver, Aneurysm [live, full]

Track 2: Lithium, Even In His Youth, Drain You [live, full], Something In The Way, Come As You Are, Polly, In Bloom, Smells Like Teen Spirit, On A Plain [live, full], Stay Away, Endless, Nameless

Track 3: Molly's Lips [live], Stain, School [live, full], Big Cheese, Been A Son, Territorial Pissings [full], Smells Like Teen Spirit [full]

CREDITS: Tracks listed are only excerpts from the full song unless otherwise stated. All the live tracks are produced and engineered by Andy Wallace and recorded live on the Dogfish Mobile Truck at the Paramount Theater, Seattle on October 31, 1991. The live versions of 'Drain You' and 'School' are the same recordings as on the 'Come As You Are' single.

US PROMOS BOX
1992

2 CD Box Set on Geffen (VD-PRO-4382/CD-PRO-4429, US) Contains Nevermind—It's An Interview and Lithium CD promos. Box is 25 x 25 x 3cm, black with hinges. Cover artwork is an egg surrounded by sperm, with a yellow Nirvana logo in the top left corner and US Promos in red in the lower right corner. Liner notes are set into the lid of the box. Only 100 produced. Comes with a CD-shaped Certificate of Authenticity.

HORMOANING
1992

12-inch on Geffen (GEF21711, Australia)
CS on Geffen (GEFC21711, Australia)
CD on Geffen (GEFD21711, Australia)

CD on DGC (MVCG-17002, Japan)
SONGS (18:51): Turnaround (2:21), Aneurysm (4:50), D-7
(3:48), Son Of A Gun (2:50), Even To His Youth (3:08),
Molly's Lips (1:52)

CREDITS: Released in January 1991. 15,000 pressed of the
Australian version (5,000 of each format). 12-inch EP is
pressed on swirled vinyl, 'Even In His Youth' and 'Aneurysm'
written by Kurt Cobain, and recorded on January 1, 1991, by
Craig Montgomery at Music Source, Seattle. 'Turnaround', 'Son
Of A Gun' and 'Molly's Lips' recorded in the UK for BBC Radio
1 John Peel Sessions. Produced by Dale Griffin. Engineered
by M. Engles and F. Kay. 'Turnaround' written by Mark
Mothersbaugh and Gerald V. Casale, (Devo). 'D-7' written by
Greg Sage (The Wipers). 'Son Of A Gun, and 'Molly's Lips'
written by Eugene Kelly and Frances McKee (The Vaselines).
Dave Grohl plays drums on all tracks.

INCESTICIDE
1992
CS on DGC (DGCC-24504, US)
CD on DGC (DGCD-24504, US)
LP on DGC (DGC-24504, US)
CD promo on DGC [LTD includes three cards] (Germany)

TRACKS: (44:45): Dive (3:53), Sliver (2:12), Stain (2:37), Been
A Son (1:53), Turnaround (2:17), Molly's Lips (1:51), Son Of A
Gun (2:47), (New Wave) Polly (1:46) Beeswax (2:47), Downer
(1:47), Mexican Seafood (1:52), Hairspray Queen (4:12), Aero
Zeppelin (4:39), Big Long Now (5:01), Aneurysm (4:36)

CREDITS: Released on December 15, 1992. Sticker on package
reads 'Rare B-Sides, BBC Sessions, Original Recordings,
Outtakes, Stuff Never Before Available'. 'Turnaround' written by
Mark Mothersbaugh and Gerald V. Casale (Devo). 'Molly's Lips'
and 'Son Of A Gun' written by Eugene Kelly and Frances McKee
(The Vaselines). 'Aneurysm' and '(New Wave) Polly' written by
Kurt Cobain, Chris Novoselic and Dave Grohl. 'Mexican Seafood'
and 'Hairspray Queen' written by Kurt Cobain. Dan Peters plays
drums on 'Sliver'. Chad Channing plays drums on 'Dive', 'Stain',

'Mexican Seafood', 'Hairspray Queen', 'Aero Zeppelin' and 'Big
Long Now'. Dale Crover plays drums on 'Downer'. Dave Grohl
plays drums on 'Been A Son', 'Turnaround', 'Molly's Lips', 'Son Of
A Gun', '(New Wave) Polly' and 'Aneurysm', 'Turnaround', 'Molly's
Lips' and 'Son Of A Gun, recorded in the UK for BBC Radio 1
John Peel Sessions.
Produced by Dale Griffin. Engineered by M. Engles and F. Kay.
'Been A Son', (New Wave) Polly" and 'Aneurysm' recorded in the UK
for BBC Radio 1 Mark Goodier Sessions. Produced by Miti Adhikari.
Engineered by John Taylor. All other Tracks written by Kurt Cobain
and Chris Novoselic. Art direction by Robert Fisher, cover painting
by Kurt Cobain. Live photograph by Charles Peterson.

IN UTERO
1993
LP on Geffen (GEF24536, UK)
CS on Geffen (GEF24536, UK)
CD on Geffen (GEFCD24536, UK)
LP on Geffen (GEF24536, Australia)
CS on Geffen (GEFC24536, Australia)
CD on Geffen (GEFD24536, Australia)

TRACKS (69:05): Serve The Servants (3:54), Scentless
Apprentice (3:47), Heart-Shaped Box (4:39), Rape Me (2:49),
Frances Farmer Will Have Her Revenge On Seattle (4:07),
Dumb (2:29), Very Ape (1:55), Milk It (3:52), Pennyroyal Tea
(3:36), Radio Friendly Unit Shifter (4:49), Tourette's (1:33),
All Apologies...Gallons Of Rubbing Alcohol Flow Through The
Strip (3:50+7:33=31:32)

LP on DGC (GDC-24607, US)
CS on DGC)DGCC-24607, US)
CD on DGC (DGCD-24607, US)

TRACKS: (41:20): Serve The Servants (3:54), Scentless Apprentice
(3:47), Heart-Shaped Box (4:39), Rape Me (2:49), Frances Farmer
Will Have Her Revenge On Seattle (4:07), Dumb (2:29), very Ape
(1:55), Milk It (3:52), Pennyroyal Tea (3:36), Radio Friendly Unit
Shifter (4:49), Tourette's (1:33), All Apologies (3:50)
CREDITS: Released on September 14, 1993 in the UK and

Australia. Released on September 21, 1993 in the U.S. 'Gallons Of Rubbing Alcohol Flow Through The Strip' is listed on non-US pressings as a 'Devalued American Dollar Purchase Incentive Track'. Dave Grohl plays drums on all tracks. All Tracks written by Kurt Cobain, except 'Scentless Apprentice' written by Kurt Cobain, Krist Novoselic and Dave Grohl. Recorded by Steve Albini in March 1993 at Pachyderm Studios in Minnesota. Technician: Bob Weston. Additional mixing on 'Heart-Shaped Box' and 'All Apologies' by Scott Litt. Second engineer with Scott Litt: Adam Kasper.

MTV UNPLUGGED IN NEW YORK
1994
LP on DGC (DGC24727, US)
CS on DGC (DGCC24727, US)
CD on DGC (DGCD24727, US)
LP on Geffen (GEF-24727, US)
CS on Geffen (GEFC-24727, US)
CD on Geffen (GEFD-24727, US)

TRACKS (53:59): About A Girl (3:37), Come As You Are (4:14), Jesus Doesn't Want Me For A Sunbeam (4:37), The Man Who Sold The World (4:21), Pennyroyal Tea (3:41), Dumb (2:53), Polly (3:16), On A Plain (3:45), Something In The Way (4:02), Plateau (3:38), Oh Me (3:26), Lake Of Fire (2:56), All Apologies (4:23), Where Did You Sleep Last Night (5:08)

CREDITS: Released on October 31, 1994. 'Jesus Doesn't Want me For A Sunbeam' written by Eugene Kelly and Frances McKee (The Vaselines). 'The Man Who Sold The World' written and originally performed by David Bowie. 'Plateau', 'Oh Me' and 'Lake Of Fire' written by Curt (The Meat Puppets). 'Where Did You Sleep Last Night' written by Huddie Ledbetter (Leadbelly). All other Tracks written by Kurt Cobain. Krist Novoselic plays bass, accordian on 'Jesus Doesn't Want Me For A Sunbeam', and guitar on 'Plateau', 'Oh Me' and 'Lake Of Fire'. Dave Grohl plays drums and vocals, bass on 'Jesus Doesn't Want Me For A Sunbeam'. Pat Smear plays guitar on all tracks. Lori Goldston plays cello on 'Jesus Doesn't Want Me For A Sunbeam', 'The Man Who Sold The World', 'Dumb', 'Polly', 'On A Plain', 'Something In The Way', 'All Apologies' and 'Where Did You Sleep Last Night'. Curt Kirkwood plays guitar on 'Plateau', 'Oh

Me' and 'Lake of Fire'. Cris Kirkwood plays guitar and backing vocals on 'Plateau' and 'Oh Me', and 'Lake Of Fire'. Recorded for MTV's Unplugged at Sony Studios, New York on November 18, 1993. Produced by Nirvana and Scott Litt. Mixed at Louie's Clubhouse. Art direction and design by Robert Fisher. Photography by Jennifer Youngblood-Grohl and Frank Micelotta.

SINGLES

LOVE BUZZ
1988
7-inch on Sub Pop (SP23, US)

TRACKS: Love Buzz, Big Cheese

CREDITS: Released in October 1988. Sub Pop Singles Club #1. 'Love Buzz' written by Robby Van Leeuwen (Shocking Blue). 'Big Cheese' written by Kurt Cobain. Chad Channings plays drums on all tracks. Only 1,000 copies released on black vinyl, individually hand-numbered.

BLEW
1989
12-inch on Tupelo (TUP EP8, UK)

TRACKS: (11:35): Blew (2:54), Love Buzz (3:34), Been A Son (2:20), Stain (2:38)

CREDITS: Released in December 1989. 'Been A Son' and 'Stain' written by Kurt Cobain and Chris Novoselic, recorded and produced by Steve Fisk at Music Source, Seattle in late summer 1989. 'Blew' written by Kurt Cobain and recorded in Seattle at Reciprocal Recordings by Jack Endino in December 1988. 'Love Buzz' written by Robby Van Leeuwen (Shocking Blue).

SLIVER
1990
7-inch on Sub Pop (SP73, US)
7-inch on Tupelo (TUP25, UK)
TRACKS: Sliver, Dive

1991

12-inch on Tupelo (TUP EP25, UK)

TRACKS: Sliver, Dive, About A Girl (live)

CDS on Tupelo (TUP CD25, UK)

TRACKS: (11:34): Sliver (2:12), Dive (3:53), About A Girl (live 2:29), Spanks Through (live 2:58) Sub Pop 7 released in September 1990. Tupelo versions of the single were released later in January 1991, due to pressing difficulties. First 3,000 copies of the Sub Pop 7 were pressed on either blue-marbled or pink vinyl. The first 2,000 copies of the Tupelo 7 were pressed on green vinyl. The Tupelo CD contains no credits, nor is the Tupelo company mentioned on the CD packaging. 'Dive' and 'Sliver' written by Kurt Cobain and Chris Novoselic. 'About A Girl' and 'Spank Thru' written by Kurt Cobain. Dan peters plays drums on 'Sliver'. Chad Channing plays drums on 'Dive'. 'Sliver' recorded on January 11, 1990, at Reciprocal Recordings, Seattle,, by Jack Endino, during Tad's lunch break. Dive recorded and produced at Smart Studios, Wisconsin in April 1990 by Butch Vig.

CANDY/MOLLY'S LIPS
(FLUID/NIRVANA SPLIT SINGLE)
1991

7-inch on Sub Pop (SP97, US)

TRACKS: Candy (live) [Fluid], Molly's Lips (live) [Nirvana]

CREDITS: Released in January 1991. Limited edition of 7,500. First 4,000 copies pressed on green-swirled vinyl, the next 3,500 pressed on black vinyl. Sub Pop Singles Club #27. 'Molly's Lips' written by Eugene Kelly and Frances McKee (The Vaselines)

HERE SHE COMES NOW/VENUS IN FURS
(NIRVANA/THE MELVINS SPLIT SINGLE)
1991

7-inch on Communion Records (Communion 23, US)
TRACKS: Here She Comes Now [Nirvana], Venus In Furs [The Melvins]

CREDITS: "Here She Comes Now' and 'Venus In Furs' written by Lou Reed (Velvet Underground). 'Here She Comes Now' recorded at Laundry Room Studios by Barret Jones in 1990. Dave Grohl plays drums on 'Here She Comes Now'.

SMELLS LIKE TEEN SPIRIT
1991

7-inch on DGC (DGCCS7, US)
CSS on DGC (DGCCS-19050, US)

TRACKS: Smells Like Teen Spirit (edit), Even In His Youth

12-inch DGC (DGCS-21673, US)
CSS on DGC (DGCSS-21673, US)
CDS on DGC (DGCDS-21673, US)

TRACKS (12:32): Smells Like Teen Spirit (edit 4:30), Even In His Youth ((4:20), Aneurysm (4:44)

7-inch on DGC (DGC5, UK)
CSS on DGC)DGCS5, UK)

TRACKS: Smells Like Teen Spirit (edit), Drain You

12-inch on DGC (DGCT5, UK)

TRACKS: Smells Like Teen Spirit (edit), Drain You, Even In His Youth

12-inch PD on DGC (DGCTP5, UK)

TRACKS: Smells Like Teen Spirit, Drain You, Aneurysm
CDS on DGC (DGCCD5, UK)
TRACKS: (17:18): Smells Like Teen Spirit (edit 4:30), Drain You (3:44), Even In His Youth (4:20), Aneurysm (4:44)

CD promo on DGC (DGC PRO-CD-4308, US)

TRACKS (9:31): Smells Like Teen Spirit (edit 4:30), Smells Like Teen Spirit (5:01)

CREDITS: Released on September 10, 1991. All Tracks written by Kurt Cobain and Nirvana. Dave Grohl plays drums on all tracks. 'Smells Like Teen Spirit' and 'Drain You' produced and engineered by Butch Vig and Nirvana. Recorded in May-June 1991 at Sound City Studios in Van Nuys, California. 'Even In His Youth' and 'Aneurysm' recorded on January 1, 1991 by Craig Montgomery at Music Source, Seattle. All tracks mixed by Andy Wallace.

ON A PLAIN
1991
CD promo on DGC (DGC CD-PRO-4354, US)

TRACKS: On A Plain (3:14)

CREDITS: On A Plain written by Kurt Cobain and Nirvana

COME AS YOU ARE
1992
12-inch promo on DGC (DGC-PRO-A-4416, US)
CD promo on DGC (DGC CD-PRO-4375, US)

TRACKS: Come As You Are (3:38)

7-inch on DGC (DGC7, UK)
7-inch on DGC (GES-19065, Germany)
CSS on DGC (DGCCS19065, Australia)

TRACKS: Come As You Are, Endless, Nameless

7-inch on DGC (DGCCS7, US)
7-inch on DGC (GES-19120, France)

TRACKS: Come As You Are, Drain You (live)

12-inch on DGC (DGC7, UK)
12-inch on DGC (DGCTP7, UK)

TRACKS: Come As You Are, Endless, Nameless, School (live)

12-inch on DGC (GET-21699, Australia)
12-inch PD on DGC (GET-21712, Germany)
12-inch on DGC (GET-21699, Germany)

TRACKS: Come As You Are, Endless, Nameless, Drain You (live)

CDS on DGC (DGCTD7, UK)

TRACKS: 4 at 15:29 Come As You Are (3:38), Endless, Nameless (6:45), School (live 2:31), Drain You (live 3:35)

12-inch on DGC (DGCS-21707, US)
CSS on DGC (DGCCS-21707, US)
CDS on DGC (DGCDS-21707, US)

TRACKS: Come As You Are (3:38), School (live 2:31), Drain You (live 3:35)

CREDITS: Released in February 1992. All tracks written by Kurt Cobain and Nirvana. Dave Grohl plays drums on all tracks. 'Come As You Are' and 'Endless, Nameless' produced and engineered by Butch Vig and Nirvana. Recorded in May-June 1991, at Sound City Studios on Van Nuys, California. 'School' and 'Drain You' recorded live on the Dogfish Mobile Truck at the Paramount Theater, Seattle, Washington, on 31 October 1991. All tracks mixed by Andy Wallace.

LITHIUM
1992
CD promo on DGC (DGC CD-PRO-4429, US)

TRACKS: Lithium (4:16)

12-inch DGC (DGCS-21815, US)
CSS on DGC (DGCCS-21815, US)
CDS on DGC (DGCDM-21815, US)
12-inch PD on DGC (DGCTP9, UK)
CSS on DGC (DGCSS-19134, Australia)

12-inch on DGC (GET-21815, Germany)

TRACKS: (9:53): Lithium (4:16), Been A Son (live 2:14), Curmudgeon (2:58)
CDS on DGC (DGCT9, UK)

TRACKS (13:42): Lithium (4:16), Been A Son (live 2:14), D-7 (3:48), Curmudgeon (2:58)

CREDITS: Released on July 20, 1992 in the UK and Australia. released on July 21, 1992 in the US. 'Lithium' produced and engineered by Butch Vig and Nirvana. Recorded in May-June 1991 at Sound City Studios in Van Nuys, California. 'Been A Son' produced and engineered by Andy Wallace and recorded live on the Dogfish Mobile Truck at the Paramount Theater, Seattle, Washington, on October 31, 1991. 'Curmudgeon' recorded in April 1992 at the Laundry Room Studios by Barret Jones. All Tracks written by Kurt Cobain and Nirvana. Dave Grohl plays drums on all tracks. US CD version comes in jewelbox case containing booklet with all lyrics for the *Nevermind* album. Picture on the back of book is ultrasound image of Frances Bean Cobain 'in utero'.

IN BLOOM
1992
7-inch on Geffen (GEF34, UK)
CSS on Geffen (GEFCS-19097, Australia)

TRACKS: In Bloom, Polly (live)

7-inch on Geffen (GFS34, UK)

TRACKS: In Bloom, Sliver (live)
12-inch on Geffen (GFST34, UK)
CDS on Geffen (GFSTD 34, UK)
CDS on Geffen (GEFDM-217"60, UK)

TRACKS (9:10): In Bloom (4:15), Sliver (live 2:03), Polly (live 2:46)

1993
CD promo on DGC (DGC PRO CD-4463-2, US)

TRACKS: In Bloom, (4:15)

CREDITS: 7-inch and cassette single released on November 30, 1992. 12-inch and CD singles released on December 7, 1992. 'In Bloom' produced and engineered by Butch Vig and Nirvana. Recorded in May-June 1991 at Sound City Studios in Van Nuys, California 'Sliver' and 'Polly' recorded live by Westwood One at O'Brien Pavillion, Del Mar, California on December 28, 1991. All tracks written by Kurt Cobain and Nirvana. Dave Grohl plays drums on all tracks.

PUSS/OH, THE GUILT
(THE JESUS LIZARD/NIRVANA SPLIT SINGLE)
1993
7-inch on Touch and Go (TG83, US)
CSS on Touch and Go (TG83CS, US)
CDS on Touch and Go (TG83CD, US)
7-inch on Touch and Go (TG83, UK)
CDS on Touch and Go (TG83CD, UK)
7-inch PD on Insipid Vinyl (IV23, Australia)

TRACKS (6:44): Puss (3:19), Oh, The Guilt (3:23)

CREDITS: Released on February 22, 1993. Limited edition of 200,000 copies worldwide. Australian picture disc is a limited edition of 1,500. UK 7-inch is a limited edition pressed on blue vinyl, some come with a free poster. 'Oh, The Guilt' written by Kurt Cobain. 'Oh, The Guilt' recorded in April 1992 at the Laundry Room Studios by Barrett Jones.

HEART-SHAPED BOX
1993
7-inch on Geffen (GFS54, UK)

TRACKS: Heart-Shaped Box, Marigold

12-inch on Geffen (GFST54, UK)
CDS on Geffen (GFSTD54, UK)
CDS on Geffen (GEFDM-21849, Australia)
CSS on Geffen (GEFCS-19191, Australia)

TRACKS: (11:10): Heart-Shaped box (4:39), Milk It (3:52),
Marigold (2:33)

12-inch promo on DGC (DGC-PRO-A-4558, US)

TRACKS: Heart-Shaped Box, gallons Of Rubbing Alcohol Flow
Through The Strip

CD promo on DGC (PRO-CD-4545, US)
CD promo on DGC (GED-21849, UK)

TRACKS: Heart-Shaped Box (4:30)

CREDITS: Released on August 23, 1993. Recorded by Steve
Albini in March 1993 at Pachyderm Studios in Minneapolis,
Minnesota. Additional mixing on 'Heart-Shaped Box' by Scott
Litt. Only available on import in the US

ALL APOLOGIES/RAPE ME
1993

7-inch on Geffen (GFS66, UK)
12-inch on Geffen (GFST66, UK)
CDS on Geffen (GFSTD66, UK)

TRACKS (10:16): All Apologies (3:50), Rape Me (2:49), MV (3:33)

CSS on Geffen (GEF FCS-21880, Australia)
CDS on Geffen (GEFDM-21880, Australia

TRACKS (10:16): All Apologies (3:50), Rape Me (2:49), Moist
Vagina (3:33)

CREDITS: Released in December 1993. 'MV' is the same song
as 'Moist Vagina', but with a censored name. Recorded by
Steve Albini in March 1993 at Pachyderm Studios in
Minneapolis, Minnesota. Additional mixing on 'All Apologies'
by Scott Litt.

ABOUT A GIRL
1994

CDS on Geffen (GEFDS-21958, Australia)
CDS on Geffen (Holland)

TRACKS: (7:15): About A Girl (3:36), Something In The Way
(3:37)

CREDITS: Released on October 24, 1994. Limited edition of
5,000, only released in Australia and Holland. Both tracks
written by Kurt Cobain, and feature Dave Grohl on drums and
Pat Smear on guitar. Lori Goldston plays cello on 'Something
In The Way'. Produced by Nirvana and Scott Litt. Mixed at
Louie's Clubhouse. Recorded for MTV's Unplugged at Sony
Studios, New York on November 18, 1993. Art direction and
design by Robert Fisher. Photography by Jennifer
Youngblood-Grohl and Frank Micelotta.

CHRONOLOGY

1965
May 5: Krist Anthony Novoselic born to Krist and Maria Novoselic.

1967
January 31: Chad Channing born to Wayne and Burnyce Channing.
February 20: Kurt Donald Cobain born to Wendy and Donald Cobain.

1969
January 14: David Eric Grohl born to James And Virginia Grohl.

1975
Kurt's parents divorce, Kurt lives with mother.

1978
Kurt's father remarried.

1979
Krist's family moves to Aberdeen.

1980
Krist's sent to Croatia for a year to live with relatives.

1981
Kurt gets his first guitar.

1983
Krist graduates from high school.

1984
May: Kurt's mother remarried to Pat O'Connor.

1985
May: Kurt drops out of high school.

1988
January 23: Nirvana records demo with Dale Crove.
October 30: Kurt smashes his first guitar.
November: 'Love Buzz'/'Big Cheese' single released.

1989
February: After recording *Bleach*, Nirvana do a short West Coast tour.
June: *Bleach* released.
June 22: The tour for *Bleach* begins in San Francisco.
September: Make up tour dates due to the loss of Jason; 'Blew', EP Recorded.
October 20: Nirvana plays first European show, Newcastle, England.

December 30: Krist and Shelli get married in Tacoma.

1990
February: Nirvana begins another short US tour.
March: After losing Chad, they play a seven-show West Coast tour.
April 10: Highly bootlegged Blind Pig Concert.
July: 'Sliver' single recorded.
September: 'Sliver' single released.
September 22: The Motor Sports show, Dan Peters's only show with Nirvana.

1991
January 1: Studio session to record 'Anuerysm' and 'Even In His Youth'.
April 17: Nirvana first plays 'Smells Like Teen Spirit'.
April 30: Nirvana formally signs with DGC/Geffen Records.
May: Started recording *Nevermind*.
August: The massive European Tour begins.
August: The video for 'Smells Like Teen Spirit' is made.
September 13: The release party for *Nevermind*.

September 20: Tour for *Nevermind* begins in Toronto.

September 24: *Nevermind* is released and debuts at No.44 on *Billboard* Chart.

October 25: 10-25-91 Kurt and Krist tape interview for Headbangers Ball.

November 2: European tour for *Nevermind* begins in Bristol, England.

November 19: Highly bootlegged Rome concert.

December: US tour with Pearl Jam and Red Hot Chili Peppers.

1992

January 10: Nirvana plays in the MTV studios.

January 11: Nirvana plays *Saturday Night Live, Nevermind* hits No.1.

January 24: Nirvana begins a world tour.

January: 'Hormoaning' released in Australia and Japan.

January: 'Come As You Are' video is made.

February 24: Kurt Cobain married Courtney Love in Waikiki, Hawaii.

June 22: Kurt collapses in Belfast due to stomach problems.

July 21: 'Lithium' single released with *Nevermind* lyric sheet.

August 19: Francis Bean Cobain is born.

August 30: Nirvana play Reading Festival .

September: Nirvana play 'Lithium' at MTV music awards, wins two awards.

November: 'In Bloom' Video hits MTV.

December 15: *Incesticide* released.

1993

March: *In Utero* recorded in two weeks .

April 9: Nirvana play benefit gig for Bosnian Rape victims.

May: 'Sliver' video hits MTV.

September: Nirvana win Best Alternative Video award at MTV Video awards.

September 14: *In Utero* released in UK.

September 19: 'Heart Shaped Box' video premieres.

September 21: After a week delay, *In Utero* released in US.

September 25: Nirvana play *Saturday Night Live* for a second time.

October 10: Nirvana begins tour promoting *In Utero*.

November 13: Nirvana records *Unplugged* session for MTV.

December 12: 'All Apologies' video hits MTV.

December 16: Nirvana *Unplugged* airs on MTV.

December 31: MTV's New Year's Eve special airs, Nirvana headlines.

1994

February: Nirvana European Tour.

February 29: The Final Nirvana show is played in Munich.

March 4: Kurt Cobain is hospitalized after a suicide attempt.

March 5: Kurt awakens from coma, asks for milkshake/swears at someone.

March 8: Kurt leaves hospital under his own power.

April 8: The body of Kurt Cobain is found. Kurt committed suicide three days previously.

April 10: Memorial Service held in Seattle, Courtney reads from Kurt's suicide note.

November 1: Nirvana: *Unplugged* in New York is released in the US.

INDEX

A

Afghan Whigs, the, 117
Albini, Steve, 78, 81, 82, 88

B

Babes In Toyland, 52
Bain Dramage, 36, 37
Bjelland, Kat, 52, 109
Black Sabbath, 8
Bowie, David, 8, 24
Brown Cow, 12
Burroughs, William S. 76
Butthole Surfers, the, 43, 49, 102

C

Carlson, Dylan, 101
Channing, Burnyce, 17
Channing, Chad
  background of, 17
  is sacked, 29
Channing, Wayne, 17
Clarke, Victoria, 78
Cobain, Donald, 8
Cobain, Frances Bean, 73
Cobain, Kurt
  birth of, 8;
  background of, 9
  on prejudice, 49
  marries Courtney, 66
  and drugs, 74, 78
  in coma, 98-100
  commits suicide, 104
Cobain, Mary, 8
Cobain, Wendy, 8, 9
Coil, 76
Collins, Brit, 78
Cope, Julian, 51
Corgan, Billy, 44
Cox, Alex, 53

D

Devo, 24, 75
Dulli, Greg, 117
Duncan, John, 84

E

Everman, Jason, 19, 20

F

Farmer, Frances, 67-70, 89
Fecal Matter, 10, 11

Finch, Jennifer, 52, 53
Fish, Steve, 23
Foo Fighters, The, 117
Freak Baby, 34

G

Geffen, 27, 41, 49, 74, 88, 107, 114–115
Gold Mountain, 41
Goldsmith, William, 117
Gordon, Kim, 27
Grant, Tom, 101
Green River, 63, 64
Grohl, David
  joins Nirvana, 29
  background of, 30
  solo projects, 44, 54, 81
  on In Utero, 88
  after Nirvana, 117
Grover, Dale, 9, 12, 14, 18
Grunge, 64–65
Guns N'Roses, 74–75

H

Hokanson, Greg, 10
Hole, 27, 51, 53, 56, 103, 115

K

K Records, 10
Kasper, Damien, 114

L

L7, 29, 52
Lavine, Michael, 83, 84
Litt, Scott, 82
Love, Courtney, 27, 43, 44, 50, 53, 56,
  62, 66, 70, 71, 103, 109
Lukin, Matt, 8, 75

M

Marander, Tracy, 10, 21, 23 41
McFedden, Bob, 11, 13
Melvins, the, 9, 10, 29
Mendal, Nate, 117
Mission Impossible, 35, 117
Moore, Thurston, 27
MTV, 32, 74, 78, 107
Mudhoney, 24, 26, 29, 63, 64, 75

N

NME, 62
Nirvana

  definition of, 6
  first incarnation of, 16
  second album, 59-61
  Unplugged broadcast, 92-93
  headline Lollapalooza, 95
Novoselic Krist (Chris)
  background of, 9, 10
  on Croatia, 82
  after Nirvana, 116
Novoselic, Krist, 9
Novoselic, Maria, 9
Novoselic, Shelly, 26, 67

O

O'Connor, Patrick, 9
Ono, Yoko, 99
Osbourne, Buzz, 8, 10, 12, 29, 41

P

Pearl Jam, 62, 116
Peters, Dan, 29
Peterson, Charles, 21
Punk, 30–34

R

Rose, Axl, 74

S

Scream, 29, 36–41
Sellouts, the, 13
Shephard, Ben, 18
Simon Ritchie Group, the, 81
Smashing Pumpkins, 44
Smear, Pat, 84, 117
Sonic Youth, 27, 41, 61
Soundgarden, 18
Stiff Woodies, 12
Sub Pop, 16, 18–19, 21, 24–25, 29,
  63–64, 117
Sugar Baby Doll, 52, 53
Tad, 24, 26
Teardrop Explodes, the, 51

V

Vaselines, the, 24, 73
Vedder, Eddie, 62, 99, 116
Vig, Butch, 29, 43